EDUCATION IN A COMPETITIVE AND GLOBALIZING WORLD SERIES

NATIONAL FINANCIAL LITERACY STRATEGY

EDUCATION IN A COMPETITIVE AND GLOBALIZING WORLD SERIES

Success in Mathematics Education
Caroline B. Baumann
2009. ISBN: 978-1-60692-299-6

Mentoring: Program Development, Relationships and Outcomes
Michael I. Keel (Editor)
2009. ISBN: 978-1-60692-287-3

Mentoring: Program Development, Relationships and Outcomes
Michael I. Keel (Editor)
2009. ISBN: 978-1-60876-727-4 (Online Book)

Motivation in Education
Desmond H. Elsworth (Editor)
2009. ISBN: 978-1-60692-234-7

Evaluating Online Learning: Challenges and Strategies for Success
Arthur T. Weston (Editor)
2009. ISBN: 978-1-60741-107-9

Enhancing Prospects of Longer-Term Sustainability of Cross-Cultural INSET Initiatives in China
Chunmei Yan
2009. ISBN: 978-1-60741-615-9

Reading at Risk: A Survey of Literary Reading in America
Rainer D. Ivanov
2009. ISBN: 978-1-60692-582-9

Reading: Assessment, Comprehension and Teaching
Nancy H. Salas and Donna D. Peyton (Editors)
2009. ISBN: 978-1-60692-615-4

Reading: Assessment, Comprehension and Teaching
Nancy H. Salas and Donna D. Peyton (Editors)
2009. ISBN: 978-1-60876-543-0 (Online Book)

Multimedia in Education and Special Education
Onan Demir and Cari Celik
2009. ISBN: 978-1-60741-073-7

Rural Education in the 21st Century
Christine M.E. Frisiras (Editor)
2009. ISBN: 978-1-60692-966-7

Nutrition Education and Change
Beatra F. Realine (Editor)
2009. ISBN: 978-1-60692-983-4

The Reading Literacy of U.S. Fourth-Grade Students in an International Context
Justin Baer, Stéphane Baldi, Kaylin Ayotte,Patricia J. Gree and Daniel McGrath
2009. ISBN: 978-1-60741-138-3

Teacher Qualifications and Kindergartners' Achievements
Cassandra M. Guarino, Laura S. Hamilton, J.R. Lockwood, Amy H. Rathbunand Elvira Germino Hausken
2009. ISBN: 978-1-60741-180-2

PCK and Teaching Innovations
Syh-Jong Jang
2009. ISBN: 978-1-60741-147-5

IT- Based Project Change Management System
Faisal Manzoor Arain and Low Sui Pheng
2009. ISBN: 978-1-60741-148-2

Learning in the Network Society and the Digitized School
Rune Krumsvik (Editor)
2009. ISBN: 978-1-60741-172-7

Effects of Family Literacy Interventions on Children's Acquisition of Reading
Ana Carolina Pena (Editor)
2009. ISBN: 978-1-60741-236-6

Approaches to Early Childhood and Elementary Education
Francis Wardle
2009. ISBN: 978-1-60741-643-2

Academic Administration: A Quest for Better Management and Leadership in Higher Education
Sheying Chen (Editor)
2009. ISBN: 978-1-60741-732-3

Recent Trends in Education
Borislav Kuzmanović and Adelina Cuevas (Editors)
2009. ISBN: 978-1-60741-795-8

Expanding Teaching and Learning Horizons in Economic Education
Franklin G. Mixon, Jr. and Richard J. Cebula
2009. ISBN: 978-1-60741-971-6

New Research in Education: Adult, Medical and Vocational
Edmondo Balistrieri and Giustino DeNino (Editors)
2009. ISBN: 978-1-60741-873-3

Disadvantaged Students and Crisis in Faith-Based Urban Schools
Thomas G. Wilson
2010. ISBN: 978-1-60741-535-0

Delving into Diversity: An International Exploration of Issues of Diversity in Education
Vanessa Green and Sue Cherrington (Editors)
2010. ISBN: 978-1-60876-361-0

Developments in Higher Education
Mary Lee Albertson (Editor)
2010. ISBN: 978-1-60876-113-5

The Process of Change in Education: Moving from Descriptive to Prescriptive Research
Baruch Offir
2010. ISBN: 978-1-60741-451-3

Career Development
Hjalmar Ohlsson and Hanne Borg (Editors)
2010. ISBN: 978-1-60741-464-3

Adopting Blended Learning for Collaborative Work in Higher Education
Alan Hogarth
2010. ISBN: 978-1-60876-260-6

Special Education in the 21st Century
MaryAnn T. Burton (Editor)
2010. ISBN: 978-1-60741-556-5

Challenges of Quality Education in Sub-Saharan African Countries
Daniel Namusonge Sifuna and Nobuhide Sawamura
2010. ISBN: 978-1-60741-509-1

Collaborative Learning: Methodology, Types of Interactions and Techniques
Edda Luzzatto and Giordano DiMarco (Editors)
2010. ISBN: 978-1-60876-076-3

Handbook of Lifelong Learning Developments
Margaret P. Caltone (Editor)
2010. ISBN: 978-1-60876-177-7

Virtual Worlds: Controversies at the Frontier of Education
Kieron Sheehy, Rebecca Ferguson and Gill Clough (Editors)
2010. ISBN: 978-1-60876-261-3

Health Education: Challenges, Issues and Impact
André Fortier and Sophie Turcotte (Editors)
2010. ISBN: 978-1-60876-568-3

Reading in 2010: A Comprehensive Review of a Changing Field
Michael F. Shaughnessy (Editor)
2010. ISBN: 978-1-60876-659-8

Becoming an Innovative Teacher Educator:
Designing and Developing a Successful Hybrid Course
Qiuyun Lin
2010. ISBN: 978-1-60876-465-5

Sexuality Education
Kelly N. Stanton (Editor)
2010. ISBN: 978-1-60692-153-1

Sexuality Education and Attitudes
Jovan Stanovic and Milo Lalic (Editors)
2010. ISBN: 978-1-60741-662-3

What Content-Area Teachers Should Know About Adolescent Literacy
National Institute for Literacy
2010. ISBN: 978-1-60741-137-6

Educational Change
Aden D. Henshall and Bruce C. Fontanez (Editors)
2010. ISBN: 978-1-60876-389-4

Collaborative and Individual Learning in Teaching
Julien Mercie, Caroline Girard, Monique Brodeur and Line Laplante
2010. ISBN: 978-1-60876-889-9

National Financial Literacy Strategy
Toma P. Hendriks (Editor)
2010. ISBN: 978-1-60741-827-6

EDUCATION IN A COMPETITIVE AND GLOBALIZING WORLD SERIES

NATIONAL FINANCIAL LITERACY STRATEGY

TOMA P. HENDRIKS
EDITOR

Nova Science Publishers, Inc.

New York

LIBRARY OF CONGRESS CATALOGING-IN-PUBLICATION DATA

National financial literacy strategy / editor, Toma P. Hendriks.
p. cm.
Includes index.
ISBN 978-1-60741-827-6 (hbk.)
1. Finance--Study and teaching--Government policy--United States. 2. Finance, Personal--Study and teaching--Government policy--United States. I. Hendriks, Toma P.
HG152.25.N38 2009
332.071'073--dc22

2009036565

Published by Nova Science Publishers, Inc. ✧ New York

CONTENTS

PREFACE

Today's increasingly complex financial services market offers consumers a vast array of products, services, and providers to choose from to meet their financial needs. While this degree of choice provides consumers with a great number of options, it also requires that they be equipped with the information, knowledge, and skills to evaluate their options and identify those that best suit their needs and circumstances. This book explores The Financial Literacy Strategy which aims to help consumers understand how to prevent becoming involved in transactions that are financially destructive, how to avoid becoming victims of fraud, and how to exercise their consumer protection rights. Financial literacy can empower consumers to be better shoppers, allowing them to obtain goods and services at lower cost. This optimizes their household budgets, providing more opportunity to consume and save or invest. Comprehensive education can help provide individuals with the financial knowledge necessary to initiate savings plans, manage debt, and make strategic investment decisions for their retirement or their children's education. This book consists of public documents which have been located, gathered, combined, reformatted, and enhanced with a subject index, selectively edited and bound to provide easy access.

Chapter 1 - To ensure that the *National Strategy for Financial Literacy* serves its goal of improving the nation's financial literacy for all Americans, the Commission will be guided with the following definition of "financial literacy" and "financial education" based on a distillation of views derived from several sources.

Financial literacy is the ability to use knowledge and skills to manage financial resources effectively for a lifetime of financial well-being.[1]

Financial education is the process by which people improve their understanding of financial products, services and concepts, so they are empowered to make informed choices, avoid pitfalls, know where to go for help and take other actions to improve their present and long-term financial well-being.[2]

Chapter 2 - In 2003, the Financial Literacy and Education Improvement Act created the Financial Literacy and Education Commission, which comprises 20 federal agencies and which the Department of the Treasury's (Treasury) Office of Financial Education coordinates. Responding to a mandate in the act, GAO assessed the Commission's effectiveness and in December 2006 recommended that the Commission (1) incorporate additional elements into its national strategy to help it serve as a true implementation plan, measure results, and ensure accountability; (2) expand current efforts to cultivate sustainable partnerships with states, localities, nonprofits, and private entities; (3) obtain independent reviewers for the required assessments of overlap in federal activities and the availability and impact of federal materials; and (4) measure customer satisfaction with its Web site and test its usability.

This statement discusses the Commission's progress in implementing GAO's recommendations and key challenges the Commission faces. To address these objectives, GAO reviewed annual reports, meeting minutes, budget, and other information from the Commission, Treasury, and related entities, and interviewed selected representatives.

Chapter 3 - Today's increasingly complex financial services market offers consumers a vast array of products, services, and providers to choose from to meet their financial needs. While this degree of choice provides consumers with a great number of options, it also requires that they be equipped with the information, knowledge, and skills to evaluate their options and identify those that best suit their needs and circumstances. This is especially the case for populations that have traditionally been underserved by our financial system.

Financial education also is essential to help consumers understand how to prevent becoming involved in transactions that are financially destructive, how to avoid becoming victims of fraud, and how to exercise their consumer protection rights. Financial literacy can empower consumers to be better shoppers, allowing them to obtain goods and services at lower cost. This optimizes their household budgets, providing more opportunity to consume and save or invest. In addition, comprehensive education can help provide individuals with the financial knowledge necessary to create household budgets, initiate savings plans, manage debt, and make strategic investment decisions for their retirement or their children's education. Having these basic financial planning skills can help families to meet their near-term obligations and to maximize their longer-term financial well being.

In: National Financial Literacy Strategy
Editor: Toma P. Hendriks

ISBN: 978-1-60741-827-6

Chapter 1

TAKING OWNERSHIP OF THE FUTURE: THE NATIONAL STRATEGY FOR FINANCIAL LITERACY

Toma P. Hendriks

INTRODUCTION

To ensure that the *National Strategy for Financial Literacy* serves its goal of improving the nation's financial literacy for all Americans, the Commission will be guided with the following definition of "financial literacy" and "financial education" based on a distillation of views derived from several sources.

Financial literacy is the ability to use knowledge and skills to manage financial resources effectively for a lifetime of financial well-being.[1]

Financial education is the process by which people improve their understanding of financial products, services and concepts, so they are empowered to make informed choices, avoid pitfalls, know where to go for help and take other actions to improve their present and long-term financial well-being.[2]

NEW CALLS TO ACTION

In addition to the existing 26 Calls to Action published in the *Strategy* of April 2006, the Commission developed six new Calls to Action for the 2007 *Strategy*. These Calls to Action are a product of the statutorily mandated review of the *Strategy* and they highlight additional areas where the Commission wishes to concentrate its efforts. Commission members will work with each other and other entities to fulfill these objectives.

Retirement Saving

Tactic Employed: Public Awareness, Partnerships

3-3 In 2007, the Department of Labor, in partnership with a national nonprofit organization and the Internal Revenue Service, will implement a multi-faceted campaign to educate small businesses and their accountants about options for employee retirement plans. This campaign will include an interactive Web site, publications and a series of seminars.

Consumer Protection

Tactic Employed: Public Awareness

5-3 By the third quarter of 2008, the Commission will host a roundtable discussion on the inclusion of insurance issues in financial education. The Commission will publish findings from this discussion.

Coordination Efforts

Tactic Employed: Partnerships

12-2.1 The Commission will identify an independent party to conduct two assessments of Federal financial education programs and resources. The first assessment will focus on availability, use, impact and overall effectiveness of Federal programs and materials; the second will identify duplication and overlap of efforts as well as gaps. The first series of independent assessments will be completed in 2009.

12-3. By the second quarter of 2009, the Commission will conduct usability testing of, and measure customer satisfaction with, MyMoney.gov. Findings will be used to improve the Web site.

12-4. In 2007, the Commission will use MyMoney.gov to highlight existing partnerships and encourage new partnerships among public, nonprofit and private organizations.

12-5. The Office of Personnel Management and the Treasury Department will partner to establish a network of state and local government officials to improve collaboration on financial education efforts among federal, state and local levels. The first meeting of the network will be held by the third quarter of 2007.

End Notes

[1]Jump$tart Coalition. 2007. *National Standards in K-12 Personal Finance Education.*

[2] Organization for Economic Co-operation and Development. 2005. *Improving Financial Literacy: Analysis of Issues and Policies.* OECD Publishing. Paris, France.

In: National Financial Literacy Strategy
Editor: Toma P. Hendriks
ISBN: 978-1-60741-827-6

Chapter 2

FINANCIAL LITERACY AND EDUCATION COMMISSION: PROGRESS MADE IN FOSTERING PARTNERSHIPS, BUT NATIONAL STRATEGY REMAINS LARGELY DESCRIPTIVE RATHER THAN STRATEGIC

Government Accountability Office

WHY GAO DID THIS STUDY

In 2003, the Financial Literacy and Education Improvement Act created the Financial Literacy and Education Commission, which comprises 20 federal agencies and which the Department of the Treasury's (Treasury) Office of Financial Education coordinates. Responding to a mandate in the act, GAO assessed the Commission's effectiveness and in December 2006 recommended that the Commission (1) incorporate additional elements into its national strategy to help it serve as a true implementation plan, measure results, and ensure accountability; (2) expand current efforts to cultivate sustainable partnerships with states, localities, nonprofits, and private entities; (3) obtain independent reviewers for the required assessments of overlap in federal activities and the availability and impact of federal materials; and (4) measure customer satisfaction with its Web site and test its usability.

This statement discusses the Commission's progress in implementing GAO's recommendations and key challenges the Commission faces. To address these objectives, GAO reviewed annual reports, meeting minutes, budget, and other information from the Commission, Treasury, and related entities, and interviewed selected representatives.

View GAO-09-638T or key components. For more information, contact Richard J. Hillman at 202-512-8678 or hillmanr@gao.gov.

What GAO Found

The Financial Literacy and Education Commission has addressed some of GAO's recommendations and not others:

The National Strategy remains largely descriptive. GAO's 2006 report noted that the Commission's National Strategy for Financial Literacy largely was descriptive rather than strategic, generally did not include a plan for implementation, and only partially addressed or defined elements such as performance measures, resource needs, and roles and responsibilities. Revisions to the strategy made since GAO's last report include new "calls to action," but do not represent a fundamental shift in approach that incorporates specific recommendations on roles, funding, and activities. As a result, the document still does not serve as a true functional strategy.

Progress has been made in fostering partnerships. The creation of the National Financial Education Network, which focuses on the state and local level, and the President's Advisory Council on Financial Literacy, which focuses on the private and nonprofit sectors, has been a positive step toward developing mutually beneficial partnerships that are sustainable over the long term.

Independent reviews have been partially initiated. Treasury has enlisted a volunteer doctoral student to conduct independent reviews on overlap of federal activities and availability of financial literacy materials, but the student will not assess the impact of the materials, as called for in the act. Treasury staff told GAO that they used a volunteer because they lacked the funds to hire a paid professional.

Commission has measured customer satisfaction with its Web site, but has not yet tested usability. Responding to GAO's recommendation, the Commission conducted a survey of users of its MyMoney.gov Web site, although only 144 surveys were completed. The Commission has not conducted usability testing, a recommended best practice for federal public Web sites, although it says it is looking into doing so later this year.

One challenge faced by the Commission has been limited resources. It has no independent budget and Congress has not provided funds targeted to the Commission since 2005, although the Commission is able to draw upon some financial and in-kind resources from its member agencies. For the past several years, Treasury's Office of Financial Education has had about five staff members to conduct its own and Commission activities. The Commission's multiagency governance structure offers benefits—such as the ability to address crosscutting issues—but also is inherently challenging because it involves coordinating 20 individual federal agencies, each with its own set of interests, resources, and constituencies.

Mr. Chairman and Members of the Subcommittee:

Thank you for the opportunity to be here today to provide an update on the status of recommendations we made in our 2006 report that assessed the effectiveness of the Financial Literacy and Education Commission (Commission). The Commission comprises 20 federal agencies and was created in 2003 by the Financial Literacy and Education Improvement Act, which charged it with improving financial literacy and education through the development of a national strategy to promote them.[1] The act mandated that we assess the effectiveness of the Commission and in December 2006 we issued a report that included recommendations to the Commission related to its national strategy, Web site, reviews of federal activities, and development of partnerships.[2]

Today I will discuss (1) the Commission's and the Department of the Treasury's (Treasury) progress in implementing recommendations that we made in our 2006 report and (2) challenges the Commission and Treasury's Office of Financial Education (OFE) face in carrying out their missions.

To prepare this testimony, we reviewed materials that the Commission published since our last review, including its annual reports to Congress, updates and additions to its national strategy, and recent data on the usage of its Web site and telephone hotline. We also gathered and reviewed budget and staffing information for OFE and reviewed contracts and materials related to the office's multimedia campaigns. We reviewed the annual report and meeting minutes of the President's Advisory Council on Financial Literacy and the Web site, agendas, and meeting minutes of the National Financial Education Network. Finally, we interviewed Treasury staff and representatives of the President's Advisory Council on Financial Literacy and the National Financial Education Network. We conducted our work from March 2009 through April 2009 in accordance with generally accepted government auditing standards. Those standards require that we plan and perform the audit to obtain sufficient, appropriate evidence to provide a reasonable basis for our findings and conclusions based on our audit objectives. We believe that the evidence obtained provides a reasonable basis for our findings and conclusions based on our audit objectives.

BACKGROUND

Financial literacy can be described as the ability to make informed judgments and to take effective actions regarding the current and future use and management of money. It includes the ability to understand financial choices, plan for the future, spend wisely, and manage the challenges associated with life events such as a job loss, saving for retirement, or paying for a child's education. Several reports we have issued in the past few years highlight the need for financial literacy in the United States. For example:

- Last month we reported that the number of private defined benefit pension plans has declined substantially over the past two decades.[3] With more individuals being asked to take responsibility for saving for their own retirement, financial skills have become increasingly important in helping to ensure that retirees can enjoy a comfortable standard of living.

- Consumers' debt and investment options are increasingly numerous and complex and consumers have faced difficulty understanding the terms of mortgages and credit cards. For instance, interviews we conducted with 112 credit cardholders indicated that many failed to understand key aspects of their cards, including when they would be charged for late payments or what actions would cause issuers to raise rates.[4]
- Based on a survey of more than 1,500 consumers conducted for a 2005 report, we found that consumers understood the basics of credit reporting but were less aware of other important information, such as the impact of information contained in credit reports and how various behaviors impact credit scores.[5]

The Financial Literacy Act states that the Commission shall be composed of the Secretary of the Treasury and the heads of 19 other federal departments and agencies, and allows the President to appoint up to five additional members. The act requires the Commission to undertake certain activities, including (1) developing a national strategy to promote financial literacy and education for all Americans; (2) establishing a financial education Web site to provide information about federal financial literacy education programs and grants; (3) establishing a toll-free hotline; (4) identifying areas of overlap and duplication among federal activities and coordinating federal efforts to implement the national strategy; (5) assessing the availability, utilization, and impact of federal financial literacy and education materials; and (6) promoting partnerships among federal, state, and local governments, nonprofit organizations, and private enterprises. The act requires that the national strategy be reviewed and modified at least once a year. It also requires the Secretary of the Treasury to develop, implement, and pilot a national public service multimedia campaign to enhance the state of financial literacy and education in the United States. OFE provides primary support to the Commission and coordinates its efforts.

NATIONAL STRATEGY IS STILL LARGELY DESCRIPTIVE, ALTHOUGH THE COMMISSION HAS ADDRESSED SOME OTHER GAO RECOMMENDATIONS

Our 2006 report assessing the effectiveness of the Commission made several recommendations. We recommended that the Secretary of the Treasury, in concert with other agency representatives of the Commission, (1) incorporate into the national strategy additional elements to help ensure accountability and more effective results; (2) consider ways to expand upon current efforts to cultivate sustainable partnerships with nonprofit and private entities; (3) provide that the review of duplication and overlap and the evaluation of federal materials are independent and do not rely solely on agencies' self-assessments; and (4) conduct usability testing of and measure satisfaction with the My Money Web site. The Commission has addressed some of GAO's recommendations and not others.

National Strategy Remains Largely Descriptive Rather Than Strategic

In 2006, we reported that the Commission's National Strategy for Financial Literacy was a useful first step in focusing attention on financial literacy but largely was descriptive rather than strategic. The strategy was comprehensive to the extent of discussing major issues and challenges in improving financial literacy and describing financial literacy initiatives in the government, nonprofit, and private sectors. However, its recommendations were presented as "calls to action" that generally did not include a plan for implementation, and the strategy only partially addressed or defined elements such as performance measures, resource needs, and roles and responsibilities that help make national strategies effective.

Our report recommended that the Secretary of the Treasury and other agency representatives of the Commission incorporate into the national strategy (1) a concrete definition for financial literacy and education; (2) clear, specific goals, performance measures, and benchmarks; (3) the actions needed to accomplish these goals; (4) a description of the resources required; and (5) a discussion of appropriate roles and responsibilities for federal agencies and others. The Commission has implemented the first of these recommendations. In its April 2007 report to Congress, the Commission provided definitions for "financial literacy" and "financial education" to help guide the scope of its work.[6] A Treasury official noted that other organizations, such as the President's Advisory Council on Financial Literacy, have begun to use these definitions as well.

However, to date the Commission has not incorporated the other elements we recommended. The Commission updates the strategy annually and provides the revisions as an addendum to its annual report to Congress. For the most part, these revisions have consisted of newly developed "calls to action" and have not represented a fundamental shift in approach that incorporates specific recommendations on roles, funding, and activities.

For example, in general the strategy still neither sets clear and specific goals and subordinate objectives for what it seeks to achieve, nor does it set priorities or performance measures for assessing progress. Without performance measures or other evaluation mechanisms, the strategy lacks a good means of measuring its progress and holding relevant players accountable. Similarly, while the strategy discusses in general terms the types of resources that are available from different sectors, it still does not address fundamental questions about the level and type of resources that are needed to implement the national strategy. No cost estimate is provided either for the strategy as a whole or for specific initiatives or activities. Without a clear description of resource needs, policymakers lack information helpful in allocating resources and directing the strategy's implementation. As a result of these factors, the National Strategy for Financial Literacy, while beneficial in some regards, still does not serve as a true functional "strategy"—a plan of action intended to achieve specifically stated goals.

Progress Has Been Made in Fostering Partnerships

The Financial Literacy Act charged the Commission with promoting partnerships among federal agencies, state and local governments, nonprofit organizations, and private enterprises. In our 2006 report, we found that it had taken some helpful steps to promote partnerships, consisting mainly of outreach and publicity efforts, such as conducting speaking engagements and holding public meetings. To cultivate sustainable partnerships with nonprofit and private entities, in our 2006 report we recommended that the Commission consider additional ways that federal agencies could coordinate with private organizations that have wide networks of resources at the community level and facilitate the efforts of state and local governments to improve financial literacy.

National Financial Education Network

In response to our recommendation, the Commission created in April 2007 the National Financial Education Network to facilitate and advance financial education at the state and local level. Network members currently include more than 30 state agencies—such as the Alabama Securities Commission, Texas Department of Banking, and Wisconsin Office of Financial Literacy—and five local government agencies, such as the New York City Department of Consumer Affairs and the Seattle Housing Authority. More than 15 national organizations also are members, including the National League of Cities and the North American Securities Administrators Association.

The network's efforts include the following:

Development of a Web-based database to share information across entities. The National Financial Education Network Database for State and Local Governments (www.flecnationalnetwork.org) was developed by the National Association of Government Defined Contribution Administrators in consultation with the network. The site largely consists of financial literacy materials developed by network members and is intended for other network members as well as the general public.

Conferences to discuss ways of overcoming challenges. The network has held two in-person meetings. The first such meeting, called the National Financial Education Network Summit, was held in Seattle, Washington, in October 2007 and hosted by three Washington-based organizations. It discussed common challenges facing financial literacy professionals. OFE hosted the second, which was held in Washington, D.C., in July 2008, and sought to develop recommendations for overcoming these challenges. Key topics included promoting financial education in the workplace, foreclosure prevention and asset preservation, and the advantages and disadvantages of mandating financial education in school curricula.

Conducting conference calls. The network has held quarterly conference calls, which usually include presentations by members and updates on the Web site database.

We believe that the Commission has taken a positive step in the creation of the National Financial Education Network. Our review indicates that the network has been a useful initial action to foster communication and collaboration among federal, state, and local entities that share the common goal of improving financial literacy. In particular, network representatives with whom we spoke felt that the network provided an opportunity for members to learn what other states and localities were doing and share best practices. At the same time, the National Financial Education Network is relatively new and remains a rather loosely structured enterprise. As the network progresses further, it could potentially benefit from a more structured approach. For example, representatives from two member organizations told us they believed the network could benefit from a clearer mission statement and membership criteria.

President's Advisory Council on Financial Literacy

The President's Advisory Council on Financial Literacy was created by executive order in January 2008.[7] The President and the Secretary of the Treasury tasked the council to work with the public and private sector to provide advice on ways to help increase financial education efforts for youths in school and for adults in the workplace, increase access to financial services, establish measures of national financial literacy, conduct research on financial knowledge, and help strengthen public and private-sector education programs. The council, which has a 2-year term, currently consists of 16 members who represent private corporations, nonprofit organizations, faith-based groups, state agencies, regulatory authorities, and academic institutions. During its first year, the council created five committees to focus on key areas of financial literacy: youth, the workplace, outreach, research, and underserved populations. The council receives some administrative support from OFE, although a council member and Treasury staff told us that most of the council's financial and administrative support has been provided by member organizations.

According to its 2008 annual report, the council implemented or began a number of initiatives in its first year, including the following:

- Partnered with the USA Freedom Corps (a White House initiative that seeks to foster a culture of citizenship, service, and responsibility) to create the President's Council Financial Literacy Corps, which provides a centralized resource for information on financial literacy volunteer opportunities;
- Collaborated with the U.S. Small Business Administration to establish the Office of Entrepreneurship Education, which provides entrepreneurial information and education, resources, and tools; and
- Hosted or participated in more than a dozen town hall meetings, roundtables, conferences and listening sessions, in which one or more council members met with local community, business, education, and nonprofit leaders to explore ways to enhance financial literacy in the community.

In addition, the council proposed recommendations for improving financial literacy, most of which were aimed at Congress or Treasury, and some of which were aimed at the private, nonprofit, academic, and state and local government sectors. The specific recommendations were organized around five general themes: (1) expanding and improving financial education for students from kindergarten through postsecondary education; (2) supporting the role of employers as providers and conduits of financial education to their employees; (3) increasing access to financial services for unbanked and underserved Americans; (4) identifying and promoting a standardized set of skills and behaviors that a financial education program should teach an individual; and (5) promoting more awareness of financial literacy and dedicating more resources to it.[8]

The council's term expires in January 2010. Thus far it appears that the council's efforts have been productive and beneficial, particularly in helping to focus high-level attention on financial literacy among leaders in nongovernmental sectors and in facilitating strategic alliances among federal, private, and nonprofit enterprises.

Commission Partially Initiated Our Recommendations for Independent Reviews of Federal Activities and Materials

In 2006, we reported that the Commission had helped coordinate federal financial literacy efforts by bringing together federal agencies on a regular basis and centralizing information from multiple agencies through its Web site and hotline, among other efforts. We also reported that the Commission asked federal agencies to provide information about their financial literacy activities in order to meet the Financial Literacy Act's requirement that the Commission identify and propose means of eliminating areas of overlap and duplication. Based on the agencies' responses, the Commission concluded that these efforts had minimal overlap and duplication. Similarly, to meet a requirement that it assess the availability, utilization, and impact of federal financial literacy materials, the Commission asked each agency to evaluate the effectiveness of its own materials and programs. The Commission reported that each agency deemed its programs and resources to be effective and worthy of continuance.

Because these processes in both cases lacked the benefit of assessment by a disinterested party, we recommended that the Secretary of the Treasury and the Commission provide for an independent third party to review duplication and overlap among federal activities and the availability, utilization, and impact of federal financial literacy materials. In response to these recommendations, the Commission stated in its April 2007 and April 2008 reports to Congress that it would identify an independent party to conduct assessments of both of these matters, with the first of the independent reviews to be completed in 2009.

In late 2008, Treasury signed a volunteer service agreement with a doctoral student whose field of study includes program evaluation to collect, analyze, and report available data on the availability and duplication of financial education resources that Commission agencies offered. According to Treasury staff, the final report of the doctoral candidate, who is doing the project as an unpaid volunteer, is expected in May 2009. The purpose of the evaluation is to determine the availability and duplication of program resources provided by Commission agencies. The evaluation will not address the provision of the mandate that calls for an assessment of the "impact" of federal financial literacy materials. Treasury staff told us they are using a doctoral candidate as a volunteer because they lacked the funds to hire a paid professional. They also noted that the Commission must depend on federal agencies to self-report their activities because the Commission lacks the resources to gather this information independently. As a result of these factors, the Commission will lack the full benefits of a professional assessment by a disinterested party, which could help facilitate efforts to ensure the most efficient and effective use of federal financial literacy resources.

Commission Measured Customer Satisfaction with Web Site, but Has Not Yet Tested Its Usability

The Financial Literacy Act required the Commission to establish and maintain a Web site to serve as a clearinghouse and provide a coordinated point of entry for information about federal financial literacy and education programs, grants, and materials. In October 2004, the Commission launched the My Money Web site (www.MyMoney.gov) in English- and Spanish- language versions. The site serves largely as a portal that consists of links to financial literacy and education Web sites that Commission member agencies maintain. From its inception through February 2009, the site received approximately 3,258,000 visits.[9] Usage has been increasing somewhat—for example, the site received an average of about 84,000 visits per month for the 6-month period ending February 2009, as compared with about 69,000 and 61,000 visits per month, respectively, for the 6-month periods ending March 2007 and September 2006.

In our 2006 report, we noted that the My Money site had not incorporated certain best practices recommended for federal public Web sites—such as measuring customer satisfaction and testing for usability—to ensure that visitors are able to find information efficiently and effectively. We recommended that the Secretary of the Treasury and the Commission have the Commission's Web site subcommittee (1) measure customer satisfaction, using whatever tools deemed appropriate, such as online surveys, focus groups, and e-mail feedback forms; and (2) conduct usability testing to measure the quality of users' experiences with the Commission's Web site.

In its April 2007 and April 2008 reports to Congress, the Commission said that it would implement these two recommendations by the second quarter of 2009. From mid-September through mid-December 2008, the Commission measured customer satisfaction by using a Web-based survey accessible through a link on MyMoney.gov. The survey included 16 questions, some of which asked about characteristics of the user, such as age, race, and gender, and some of which asked for the user's impressions, complaints, and suggestions about the site. Few users completed the survey—144 surveys were completed for the approximately 240,000 site visits occurring during the 3 months that the survey was available. Results of the survey are still in the process of being analyzed and Treasury staff say they will use the findings to help improve the Web site. Finally, the Commission has not implemented usability testing but, according to Treasury staff, is looking into implementing such a test later this year.

Other Communications Initiatives Are In Place

In addition to a Web site, the Financial Literacy Act also required that the Commission establish a toll-free telephone number for members of the public seeking information related to financial literacy. The Commission launched the hotline (1-888-MyMoney) in October 2004, and it serves as an order line for a free "tool kit" of publications. Usage of this hotline has been limited and does not appear to be increasing. According to data obtained from the General Services Administration (GSA), which administers the hotline, it received 513 calls in February 2009, as compared with 526 calls in March 2007, the last month for which we previously requested these data.

As part of the national strategy, the Financial Literacy Act also required the Secretary of the Treasury to develop, implement, and pilot a national public service multimedia campaign to enhance financial literacy in the United States.[10] In fiscal year 2005, the department obligated $750,000 to support this campaign, and chose to focus on credit literacy among young adults.[11] The campaign was launched in September 2008 and has included television, radio, and Web banner advertising. It encourages young adults (ages 18-24) to develop better credit and spending habits and understand the consequences of developing bad credit. The campaign also features a new Web site, www.controlyourcredit.gov, where the audience can play an online game that emphasizes the importance of maintaining good credit. Elements of the public service announcements also are available in Spanish. The media have donated advertising time and space for the announcements through the Advertising Council.

In fiscal year 2008, an explanatory statement by the Chairman of the House Committee on Appropriations of the House of Representatives specified that OFE should spend at least $200,000 for activities combating predatory lending and encouraging the use of mainstream financial services.[12] Some of this funding was used for personnel and travel costs, according to Treasury staff, but most of it went toward a $155,000 contract that Treasury signed with a media agency in September 2008. The agency will conduct a media campaign through radio, print media, and text messages that is designed to help Americans understand various financial products and services and avoid predatory practices or detrimental financial products. The text message campaign is under way and the other aspects of the campaign are scheduled to begin in the near future, according to Treasury staff. In addition, new content has been posted to the MyMoney Web site (www.mymoney.gov/borrow-smart.shtml) and printed materials were included with nearly 2 million tax refunds.

The same explanatory statement by the Chairman of the Committee on Appropriations of the House of Representatives specified in fiscal year 2008 that OFE should spend at least $200,000 toward financial education efforts aimed at elementary and high schools.[13] Treasury staff told us that the majority of these funds have been spent on implementation of the National Financial Literacy Challenge, conducted in partnership with the President's Advisory Council on Financial Literacy, in which more than 120,000 American high school students took a 35-question exam on personal finance issues in 2008. The average score was 56 percent, which the council noted was an indicator that more rigorous financial education is needed in the schools. Treasury awarded certificates and medals to students receiving high scores, and a private foundation offered college scholarships to 32 students who achieved a perfect score on the exam.

COMMISSION FACES CHALLENGES IN ACHIEVING ITS MISSION

The Financial Literacy and Education Commission has played a helpful role by serving as a focal point for federal efforts and making financial literacy a more prominent issue among the media, policymakers, and consumers. Key challenges the Commission faces include its own limited resources and a governance structure that depends on the commitment and collaboration of 20 individual agencies.

Table 1. Treasury Department Office of Financial Education Staff Support to Financial Literacy and Education Commission Activities, Estimated, Fiscal Years 2005–2009

Fiscal year	Staff years[a]
2005	2
2006	2.5
2007	2.5
2008	1.5
2009	0.75

Source: Treasury OFE.

[a]Full-time equivalent. Includes staff time devoted to the President's Advisory Council on Financial Literacy and the National Financial Education Network. Staff years for 2006- 2008 include detailees from other agencies.

Commission and OFE Have Limited Resources and Staff

While many federal agencies devote funds to financial literacy and education, the resources available specifically to the Financial Literacy and Education Commission and to Treasury's Office of Financial Education—which provides support to the Commission—have been limited.

Financial Literacy and Education Commission

The Financial Literacy Act, which created the Commission, authorized the appropriation of "such sums as may be necessary to carry out its provisions."[14] In addition, the act authorized the appropriation to the Secretary of the Treasury of $3 million for fiscal years 2004, 2005, and 2006 to develop, produce and distribute the multimedia campaign.

However, the Commission has received no direct appropriation since its inception and Treasury has never requested funds specifically for the Commission in the President's budget request for the department, according to Treasury staff. Some of the Commission's activities have been funded through appropriations provided for Treasury's Departmental Offices, Salaries, and Expenses appropriation. For example, $1 million in fiscal year 2005 of the funds appropriated to Treasury was specified for promoting basic financial literacy and education and was used in part to develop and implement the Commission's national strategy.[15]

OFE has provided the primary administrative support for the Commission and devoted a significant portion of its resources to support Commission activities. As shown in table 1, OFE estimates that in each fiscal year since 2005, it has devoted from about .75 to 2.5 staff years (full-time equivalent staff) to support the Commission and related entities, with staffing at its lowest levels during the 2 most recent fiscal years.

Other federal agencies have detailed staff members to the Commission for short periods—for example, our prior report noted that as of August 2006, the Federal Deposit Insurance Corporation, GSA, and Department of Justice had detailed seven staff members to work at OFE on Commission activities for periods ranging from 2 months to 2 years each. Member agencies have provided other in-kind staff assistance and financial resources as well. For example, GSA hosts the My Money Web site and had estimated that as of August 2006, its staff had devoted about 4,000 hours to support the site and other Commission activities. GSA's Federal Citizen Information Center covers the cost of the Commission's telephone hotline, which we previously reported was about $28,000 in fiscal year 2006. Most other representatives of the Commission could not provide us with an estimate of the resources their agencies had devoted to the Commission, most of which had consisted of in-kind staff assistance.

Office of Financial Education

Treasury's Office of Financial Education as a whole has had about five full-time equivalent staff each year during fiscal years 2005-2009, which includes the staff time devoted to activities of the Commission. Through fiscal year 2008, Treasury did not assign OFE as a separate cost center; rather, its funding was provided within Treasury's Financial Policies and Programs budget activity, which was also part of Treasury's Departmental Offices, Salaries, and Expenses appropriation. The explanatory statements accompanying Treasury's fiscal year 2008 Departmental Offices, Salaries, and Expenses appropriation directed Treasury to fund OFE at not less than $1.1 million, of which at least $200,000 each was to be used for activities—as discussed earlier—focused on (1) elementary and high schools and (2) combating predatory lending and encouraging the use of mainstream financial services.[16] Treasury began to assign a separate cost center for OFE in fiscal year 2009, allocating $1.6 million to the office, according to Treasury staff. The explanatory statement for the fiscal year 2009 appropriation act specified that OFE should target an additional $500,000 provided over its assumed budget request toward efforts aimed at elementary and high schools and combating predatory lending.[17]

Currently, compounding these resource challenges is the number of vacant leadership positions at key Treasury posts, including Deputy Assistant Secretary for Financial Education, as well as the Assistant Secretary for Financial Institutions and the Under Secretary for Domestic Finance. Filling these positions with individuals committed to improving our nation's financial literacy will be important.

Commission's Governance Structure Has Benefits but Also Creates Challenges

As noted earlier, the Financial Literacy and Education Commission is composed of a large number of agencies but is housed administratively in Treasury, has no independent budget, and has no legal authority to compel member agencies to take any action. This governance structure has advantages and disadvantages. It has the benefit of bringing together a large number of players to achieve the common goal of improving Americans' financial literacy. Achieving results for the nation increasingly requires that federal agencies work together, and it would be difficult, if not impossible, for one agency alone to address the crosscutting issue of financial literacy. The multiagency structure of the Commission also may facilitate collaboration with nonfederal entities and, indeed, Congress charged the Commission with promoting such partnerships.

At the same time, coordinating the efforts of 20 individual federal agencies is inherently challenging. Each has its own set of interests, resources, and constituencies. In prior work, we have identified barriers to coordinating programs and initiatives across the federal government, including competing missions, concerns about protecting resources, and a lack of clearly articulated roles and responsibilities.[18] As we noted in our 2006 report, these barriers may have affected the Commission's efforts to coordinate federal programs—as well as its ability to streamline federal financial literacy initiatives to make the best use of scarce resources.

Mr. Chairman, this concludes my prepared statement. I would be happy to answer any questions you or other Members of the Subcommittee may have.

End Notes

[1] The Financial Literacy and Education Improvement Act was Title V of the Fair and Accurate Credit Transactions Act of 2003, Pub. L. No. 108-159, Title V, 117 Stat. 2003 (2003) (codified at 20 U.S.C. §§ 9701–08). Hereafter, this statement refers to this act as the "Financial Literacy Act."

[2] GAO, *Financial Literacy and Education Commission: Further Progress Needed to Ensure an Effective National Strategy*, GAO-07-100 (Washington, D.C.: Dec. 4, 2006). We also provided an update to this report in a 2007 testimony, *Financial Literacy and Education Commission: Further Progress Needed to Ensure an Effective National Strategy*, GAO-07-777T (Washington, D.C.: Apr. 30, 2007).

[3] GAO, *Defined Benefit Pensions: Survey Results of the Nation's Largest Private Defined Benefit Plan Sponsors*, GAO-09-291 (Washington, D.C.: Mar. 30, 2009).

[4] GAO, *Credit Cards: Increased Complexity in Rates and Fees Heightens Need for More Effective Disclosures to Consumers*, GAO-06-929 (Washington, D.C.: Sept. 12, 2006).

[5] GAO, *Credit Reporting Literacy: Consumers Understood the Basics but Could Benefit from Targeted Educational Efforts*, GAO-05-223 (Washington, D.C.: Mar. 16, 2005).

[6] The Commission defines financial literacy as "the ability to use knowledge and skills to manage financial resources effectively for a lifetime of financial well-being" and defines financial education as "the process by which people improve their understanding of financial products, services, concepts, so they are empowered to make informed choices, avoid pitfalls, know where to go for help and take other actions to improve their present and long-term financial well-being."

[7] Exec. Order No. 13455, 73 Fed. Reg. 4445 (Jan. 22, 2008).

[8] Department of the Treasury, *President's Advisory Council on Financial Literacy: 2008 Annual Report to the President* (Washington, D.C., Jan. 6, 2009).

[9] A "visit" is defined as all the activity of one visitor to a Web site within a specified period, usually 30 minutes. Because federal government Web sites are generally prohibited from using "cookies" (small files stored on a visitor's computer that can contain identifying information about the visitor), the number of unique visitors to the My Money Web site cannot be counted. Thus, data on total number of visits do not represent the number of users who have visited the Web site because some users may visit the site multiple times. According to a General Services Administration official, because unique visitors cannot be counted, the best measure of the Web site's usage is number of visits.

[10] 20 U.S.C. § 9707.

[11] The Financial Literacy Act authorized to be appropriated $3 million for the development, production, and distribution of the campaign for fiscal years 2004, 2005, and 2006. 20 U.S.C. § 9707(f). The conference report accompanying Treasury's fiscal year 2005, Departmental Offices, Salaries, and Expenses appropriation specified that $1 million should be used to promote basic financial literacy and education. H.R. Conf. Rep. No. 108-792, at 1443 (2004). Treasury obligated $750,000 to support the multimedia campaign conducted as part of the national strategy.

[12] 153 Cong. Rec H15741, H16048 (Dec. 17, 2007). No conference report accompanied the Consolidated Appropriations Act, 2008 (2008 Appropriation Act), Pub. L. No. 110–16 1. However, the Chairman of the Committee on Appropriations of the House of Representatives had printed an explanatory statement in the *Congressional Record*. Section 4 of the 2008 Appropriation Act states that this explanatory statement should be given the same effect with respect to the allocation of funds and implementation as if it were a joint explanatory statement of a committee of conference. While legislative history such as these statements and other congressional reports generally are not legally binding, they do provide informational guidance. *See* Congressional Research Service, *Earmarks Executive Order: Legal Issues* (RL34373) (February 13, 2008). In fiscal year 2009, additional monies were specified for financial education and combating predatory lending in

a similar explanatory statement accompanying the Omnibus Appropriations Act, 2009, Pub. L. No. 111-8. *See* 155 Cong. Rec. H1653, H1988 (Feb. 23, 2009).

[13] See footnote 12.

[14] 20 U.S.C. § 9708.

[15] See footnote 11.

[16] See footnote 12. The explanatory statement states that "(1) not less than $200,000 is directed to be used to further the office's outreach and education activities focused on elementary schools and high schools, and (2) not less than $200,000 is directed to be used for the development of tailored, targeted materials and dissemination strategies to protect consumers against predatory lending and encourage the use of mainstream financial services."

[17] See footnote 12. The explanatory statement directs Treasury to fund OFE within the Financial Policies and Programs budget activity at an increased level of $500,000. "The Department is directed to target this increase toward financial education efforts aimed at elementary and high schools, as well as efforts aimed at combating predatory lending."

[18] GAO, *Managing for Results: Barriers to Interagency Coordination,* GAO/GGD-00-106 (Washington, D.C.: Mar. 29, 2000), and *Results-Oriented Government: Practices That Can Help Enhance and Sustain Collaboration among Federal Agencies,* GAO-06-15 (Washington, D.C.: Oct. 21, 2005).

In: National Financial Literacy Strategy
Editor: Toma P. Hendriks

ISBN: 978-1-60741-827-6

Chapter 3

TAKING OWNERSHIP OF THE FUTURE

Financial Literacy and Education Commission

FOREWORD PART I: TAKING OWNERSHIP OF THE FUTURE

Today's increasingly complex financial services market offers consumers a vast array of products, services, and providers to choose from to meet their financial needs. While this degree of choice provides consumers with a great number of options, it also requires that they be equipped with the information, knowledge, and skills to evaluate their options and identify those that best suit their needs and circumstances. This is especially the case for populations that have traditionally been underserved by our financial system.

Financial education also is essential to help consumers understand how to prevent becoming involved in transactions that are financially destructive, how to avoid becoming victims of fraud, and how to exercise their consumer protection rights. Financial literacy can empower consumers to be better shoppers, allowing them to obtain goods and services at lower cost. This optimizes their household budgets, providing more opportunity to consume and save or invest. In addition, comprehensive education can help provide individuals with the financial knowledge necessary to create household budgets, initiate savings plans, manage debt, and make strategic investment decisions for their retirement or their children's education. Having these basic financial planning skills can help families to meet their near-term obligations and to maximize their longer-term financial well being.

In 2003, Congress established the Financial Literacy and Education Commission (the Commission) through passage of the Financial Literacy and Education Improvement Act under Title V of the Fair and Accurate Credit Transactions (FACT) Act of 2003 (P.L. 108-159). Congress designated the Treasury Department's Office of Financial Education to lend its expertise and provide primary support to the Commission, which is chaired by the Secretary of the Treasury. In addition to the Treasury Department, the following Federal agencies are represented on the Commission: The Federal banking agencies (as defined in Section 3 of the Federal Deposit Insurance Act)—the Office of the Comptroller of the Currency (OCC), the Board of Governors of the Federal Reserve System (FRB), the Federal Deposit Insurance Corporation (FDIC), and the Office of Thrift Supervision (OTS)—the

National Credit Union Administration (NCUA), the Securities and Exchange Commission (SEC), each of the Departments of Education, Agriculture (USDA), Defense (DOD), Health and Human Services (HHS), Housing and Urban Development (HUD), Labor (DOL), and Veteran Affairs (VA), the Federal Trade Commission (FTC), the General Services Administration (GSA), the Small Business Administration (SBA), the Social Security Administration (SSA), the Commodity Futures Trading Commission (CFTC), and the Office of Personnel Management (OPM).

Congress charged the Commission to "improve the financial literacy and education of persons in the United States through development of a national strategy to promote financial literacy and education." The statute also provides for a yearly re-examination of the progress of that strategy. This document represents the first step in the evolutionary process of crafting and refining a framework for a national strategy for improving the financial literacy and education of Americans. Under the terms of the statute, the Commission will annually review the *National Strategy* and make changes and recommendations as it deems necessary.

Title V, Section 514 of the FACT Act states, in part, that the strategy "shall provide for participation by state and local governments and private, nonprofit, and public institutions in the creation and implementation of such strategy." This mandate recognizes that both the private sector and the public sector are essential to improving financial literacy in America. In adherence to this mandate, the Commission sought input from financial education providers and examined resources of the Federal, state, and local governments, nonprofit organizations, academia, and the private sector.

The Commission has met as a body every four months since it was established in January 2004, inviting representatives from an array of financial education sources to present information on particular programs to inform the Commission membership. The Commission also called for public comment on August 26, 2004, and in response, over 150 individuals and organizations replied. In an effort to obtain more information and detail from these respondents, the Commission held six sector-specific public meetings, inviting those who had submitted written comments to present more information. Many used their own resources to travel to Washington, D.C. to attend these meetings and others were able to participate by telephone. The Commission is grateful to the participants for their thoughtful comments and willingness to share knowledge and opinions. Both the *Federal Register* notice and the summaries of these meetings are included in the Appendices to the Strategy. Many of the elements in this Strategy document were contributed by meeting attendees.

It is clear that there is a myriad of ongoing financial education efforts within the United States, targeting a wide variety of topics and audiences and employing various strategies to deliver financial education. Some of the efforts that the Commission identified represent background research that was instrumental in developing a framework for the *National Strategy*. Sponsored by Federal, state, and local government agencies, private entities, nonprofit organizations, and institutions of higher learning, these and many other programs respond to the financial literacy and education needs of many different segments of our population. One fundamental challenge to improving financial education centers on reaching those who lack the awareness of the availability of such resources, who may not have the time to improve their level of financial education, or for whom existing information resources are inaccessible or inadequate. Americans may be unable to take advantage of existing educational resources for a variety of reasons, including lack of Internet access, language barriers, or because they are not the targets of traditional methods of dissemination. One major and over-arching goal of the *National Strategy*, then, must be to make it easier to access and use helpful, appropriate, and timely financial education information, in a format most useful to the intended recipient.

Another challenge that represents an opportunity for the Commission is helping Americans discern the difference between financial education and marketing. Occasionally, a company may try to deliver financial education in marketing materials for financial products or services. This may blur the distinction between the sales information and the important financial literacy points. That blurring may make it more difficult for consumers to evaluate products and determine if the information is accurate and complete or whether the provider is unbiased or whether the information provided is clouded by potential financial gain.

This is not a simple task. Personal financial management is an extremely complex matter that requires significant resources and commitment by consumers to understand and evaluate the multitude of products available in the broad financial services market. In addition, the marketplace is constantly changing, with new products, services, and providers emerging to meet consumer demand. As a result, the range of topics and issues that consumers must evaluate is vast and ever-growing. Financial education efforts should aim at helping consumers understand and select the products and services that best suit their needs, goals, and circumstances. Providing effective financial education presents great challenges not only because of the complexity of the issues surrounding the need for financial education, but also the individualistic nature of the approach necessary to address those issues. As a result, another goal of the *National Strategy* is to help consumers identify reliable and unbiased sources of information and equip them with the skills needed to choose reliable products and services.

Given the important role of financial education in promoting financial well-being, there is a long-standing commitment to financial education from government, private industry, and nonprofit organizations. Marshaling that commitment and organizing efforts to produce the best possible result is the greatest challenge of all, and one that can be addressed through a national strategy. The Commission has concluded that an effective national strategy must encompass four crucial areas, set forth below. Future evaluations of this strategy will focus upon reviewing progress in and refining the articulation of these major strategic areas.

1. Building Public Awareness of Available Resources

Improved financial literacy among all Americans requires an increased public awareness of the issues, as well as the many state, local, and national resources that are available for financial education. One theme that emerged from the Commission's sector-specific meetings was the realization that the Federal government must make its financial literacy resources more easily available. This is important in order to better leverage existing financial education resources and avoid overlap or duplication.

The Commission has established an information distribution infrastructure which will help increase public awareness of the resources available within the Federal government by establishing MyMoney.gov, a clearinghouse for financial literacy materials. This Web site contains links to free financial literacy and educational materials produced by Commission members. MyMoney.gov also provides links to selected.edu sites maintained by publicly funded colleges and universities affiliated with the USDA Cooperative State Research, Education, and Extension Service (CSREES), as well as.org sites affiliated with government entities such as the Federal Reserve Banks, to ensure that valuable financial information and learning tools are available from sites beyond Federal government agencies. The goal of the MyMoney.gov Web site is to provide a convenient and accessible source for credible and free resources. The Web site now contains useful information for individuals who are facing an array of financial needs, such as balancing a checking account, shopping for a mortgage or auto loan, researching ways to pay for a college education, reviewing credit card statements, putting money away for retirement, understanding a credit report, or simply deciding whether to pay cash or to charge a purchase. It contains information on how to understand, evaluate, and compare financial products, services, and opportunities and assists investors in understanding how to proceed when they encounter difficulties with market intermediaries. Although the Web site is arranged to be accessible and helpful to consumers, it also will make it easier for community educators and nonprofit organizations to find and use those same resources, reducing costs of needless duplication.

An immediate byproduct of the establishment of MyMoney.gov has been to more clearly identify the financial literacy resources that are currently available from Commission members. This important step will facilitate each Commission member's analysis of whether there are areas of needless overlap and duplication within this body of financial education materials. Existence of the Web site, with materials arranged by subject matter instead of by Commission member, will greatly facilitate coordination of efforts to promote financial literacy. Creation of the Commission has brought into focus the fact that financial literacy involves a multiplicity of issues that must be addressed. The Commission meetings, public comments, and sector-specific gatherings have highlighted the range of issues that are involved. Each Commission member has unique areas of expertise and will promote the various facets of financial literacy that fall within the expertise that resides in each agency. As additional materials are developed and linked to from MyMoney.gov, each Commission member can learn from and build upon the shared expertise of others.

The Commission also has established a toll-free number, 1-888-MyMoney, to disseminate a variety of educational materials found on the Web site to those who are unable or unwilling to use the Internet. By establishing one central source for all of these financial literacy and education materials, the Federal government can ensure that consumers and educators alike have easy access to accurate, up-to-date, and easy-to-find information and resources on financial matters.

Congress has charged the Secretary of the Treasury with developing, implementing, and conducting a pilot national public service multimedia campaign to enhance the state of financial literacy and education in the United States. This multimedia campaign will be an integral part of the strategy for raising public awareness of the importance of the issue and for informing Americans about where they can obtain high-quality, timely information on a wide variety of financial issues. This campaign will be an effective tool to actively market the MyMoney.gov Web site and the 1-888-MyMoney toll-free number. By using direct and creative messaging, an effective media campaign can help establish MyMoney. gov and 1-888-MyMoney as the primary portals to which consumers can turn when they need to easily find financial education materials on a wide range of important financial topics. Using this multimedia strategy, we can begin to build national awareness of the many valuable, free resources that are available to all citizens.

2. Developing Tailored, Targeted Materials and Dissemination Strategies

Fortunately, a large variety of excellent financial education materials exists. The MyMoney.gov Web site catalogs a great deal of neutral, unbiased information aimed at educating consumers, enabling them to obtain materials that can assist them in making informed financial decisions. Rather than creating new teaching materials, these existing materials and resources can be tailored for particular audiences and distributed through those organizations and dissemination channels that are most trusted within individual communities A single-source Web site, like MyMoney.gov, can help educators maximize their use of free financial education resources and eliminate needless duplication of effort.

Improving the financial literacy of Americans is not an action that occurs through a one-size-fits-all approach. People learn in many different ways, and many of us benefit from hearing and seeing educational messages repeated in many different ways on different occasions. Effective financial literacy and educational efforts require materials that reach and are clearly understood by the intended audience. Tailored, targeted resources are important to reach key demographics, including unbanked populations, multicultural and multilingual communities, geographically remote communities, and consumers with special needs. It is important to appreciate that dissemination channels differ widely according to the message and intended recipient, and what may appear to be duplication of effort is often necessary in order to reach different target audiences. Needless duplication occurs only when educators and others are unaware of the existence of useable information.

Developing a wide variety of effective channels is an important facet of the financial literacy challenge. Information can be disseminated in many settings, including the workplace, schools, media, and through community organizations. Each venue offers valuable outlets for reaching different demographic sectors.

A challenge to financial education efforts is understanding that access to information and programs does not always result in positive consumer behavior. For example, the workplace can be an important channel in dissemination of effective financial information. Access to an employer-based retirement plan offers an essential mechanism to facilitating structured savings. However, the availability of such a plan does not correlate to high participation in such plans. In 2004, only 53.4 per cent of all full-time employees participated in an employer-sponsored retirement plan. In recognition of this, in 2006, the Treasury Department and DOL will co-host a roundtable with large employers on retirement saving. Topics will include successful strategies in integrating the delivery of financial education into the workplace and other options for increasing participation and contributions in private pensions, such as automatic enrollment. In addition, the SBA, DOL, and the Treasury Department are committed to conducting outreach to small businesses, and will continue to offer valuable resources on retirement options to small firms. The SBA will make available specific information for small businesses on general retirement issues by providing and online training link that will be available on MyMoney. gov by the second quarter of 2006.

Another key component of the financial literacy challenge is to integrate financial education into established curricula for elementary, secondary, and post-secondary learning institutions. Identifying opportunities to incorporate financial education in this manner can help young Americans grow into financially educated adults who are astute consumers and who, in turn, impart this knowledge to their children. This kind of financial education can result in better household budgeting and other critical life skills. To help educators convey financial education concepts as part of core subjects such as math and reading, the Treasury Department and the Department of Education will partner to host a summit focused on financial education integration, teacher training, and related topics.

Financial issues and education vary across cultures, and acquiring an understanding of these differences is critical to increasing the role of minority markets in areas such as transaction accounts and homeownership. For some, there is a lack of trust of banks and government agencies. Others have varying attitudes toward spending and saving, and may use intra-cultural financial mechanisms such as peer lending and investing groups within their communities. Still others may adhere to religious restrictions, such as the Islamic prohibition on the payment of interest. In some communities, such as Native American reservations and ethnically concentrated neighborhoods, there may not be an abundance of financial institutions. These communities seek specific strategies to help them better secure the financial services resources, while gaining the products, underwriting, and delivery mechanisms that are culturally compatible.

Community organizations can play an important role in efforts to enhance the delivery of financial education information. For example, technology and innovation have resulted in the creation of a plethora of mortgage loan products that are complex and possess features that may be inappropriate, very risky, and financially detrimental for some consumers, such as adjustable rate mortgages and interest-only loans where payment levels can change dramatically over the term of the loan. In addition, as the mortgage lending market has become more competitive and prolific, the emergence of unscrupulous lenders has created concern regarding predatory lending practices. While some regulatory and legislative interventions have been undertaken to thwart predatory lending, financial education is a critical component of protecting homeowner equity. Community-based programs can be effective in both promoting and preserving homeownership. Local homeownership initiatives can raise awareness and move many individuals and families closer to making the dream of homeownership a reality. Similarly, intervention at a community level for homeowners in financial difficulty can help mitigate the effect of predatory lending for consumers and communities.

3. Tapping into Public-Private and Private-Private Partnerships

Improving the nation's financial literacy is not a task that can be undertaken solely by the Federal government. To the contrary, the majority of financial education and skills-building activities are those currently led by private-sector organizations. Community involvement can greatly enhance the effectiveness of collaborative resource development and dissemination efforts. Public-private and private-private partnerships therefore play an important role in equipping consumers with needed financial skills. Successful partnerships can efficiently reach key audiences with high-quality, unbiased information. These partnerships can highlight the local successes of financial literacy efforts and boost local enrollment in and access to education programs. Partnerships are valuable components to any public awareness effort initiated by the Commission, and collaboration is a key part of the *National Strategy* to improve financial literacy.

The area of homeownership is just one of many in which public-private partnerships can be particularly effective. Between the second quarter of 2006 and the first quarter of 2007, HUD will join with the Treasury Department to host a series of meetings highlighting the work of successful partnerships that have advanced homeownership.

Partnerships within communities can be effective at addressing the issues involved with the many individuals in this country who do not maintain traditional bank transaction, credit, savings, or investment accounts. The Treasury Department, along with the FDIC, the NCUA, and the OCC, will host a series of four regional conferences to share best practices on banking of the unbanked. The conferences will take place between the second quarter of 2006 and the third quarter of 2007 and will bring together community-based organizations, financial service providers, and Federal, state, and local regulators to broker partnerships and discuss the latest developments and strategies in bringing people into the financial mainstream.

Partnerships have also been effective at encouraging wealth building. Several Commission members are among multiple nonprofit groups, employers, financial institutions, and government agencies who are working in cooperative partnerships at the local, state, or national levels to encourage saving among low- and moderate-income individuals. Government participants include the FRB, OCC, SEC, DOL, and CSREES, the Federal partner in the Cooperative Extension System.

4. Research and Evaluation of Financial Education Programs

While many excellent financial education efforts are ongoing throughout the nation, a theme repeatedly sounded in public comment letters and during the Commission's sector-specific meetings is that a systematic method of evaluation of financial literacy programs does not exist. Additionally, there is little research on successful methods for financial education. A broad and deep base of research on financial education will assist policymakers, as well as public and private sector providers of financial education, to improve the effectiveness of their work on financial literacy. While some good research has been conducted, more can be done. From research comes a shared body of knowledge on how to best inform and educate different and varied constituencies on financial education topics. Such research is essential in developing and replicating programs that are proven to achieve results and to ensure the efficient use of resources.

Ideally, financial education programs would strive to incorporate findings from academic research that utilize both qualitative and quantitative measures to assess the effectiveness of financial education programs. For consumers, these data will offer confidence about programs that work; for educators, the data will offer guidelines for developing evidence- based, quality materials; and for funders of financial education, research provides assurance of the optimization of resources.

To raise awareness of existing academic research and to define what still needs study, the Treasury Department, along with the USDA and CSREES, will convene a symposium of researchers who specialize in financial education. The symposium will result in a working paper which will survey current financial education research and also will identify areas of potential future research.

CONCLUSION

The United States is not the only country in the world to be engaged in a serious analysis of the financial literacy and educational needs of its citizens. Virtually every other nation faces the same challenge to increase the financial knowledge and skill set of citizens to enable them to make better financial decisions and avoid fraud. As the process of developing *National Strategy* continues, it will be important to continue a dialogue with other nations in an effort to learn from their efforts.

Reaching the goal of a financially educated population will take time, but the Commission is encouraged by the many excellent programs and partnerships currently working to improve American financial literacy levels. Part II of this Foreword contains descriptions of representative programs now in place across America. Of necessity, this *National Strategy* contains merely a small sampling of the many fine programs in existence today. Yet each of the programs described illustrates the multitude of smaller efforts that represent opportunities for learning and partnership in contributing to the larger national mosaic that comprises America's financial literacy and education effort.

FOREWORD PART II: ILLUSTRATIVE PROGRAMS

Established to improve financial literacy and education among all Americans, the Commission was created when the Financial Literacy and Education Improvement Act under Title V of the FACT Act (P.L. 108-159) was signed into law by President George W. Bush on December 4, 2003.

The Commission was charged by the U.S. Congress to "improve the financial literacy and education of persons in the United States through the development of a national strategy to promote financial literacy and education."

The principal duties of the Commission include:

1. Encouraging government and private sector efforts to promote financial literacy;
2. Coordinating financial education efforts of the Federal government;
3. Developing a national strategy to promote financial literacy and education among all Americans;
4. Establishing a national financial education Web site to provide a coordinated point of entry for information about federal financial literacy, education programs, and grants; and
5. Establishing a toll-free hotline available to the public seeking materials on issues pertaining to financial literacy and education.

Programs Discussed in this Report

In each of the 13 chapters included in the *National Strategy*, the Commission delved into issues, many identified by Congress, pertinent to financial education. Each chapter describes various financial education programs developed and managed by nonprofit organizations, academia, the Federal, state, and local governments, and the private sector. The "Calls to Action" identified at the end of each chapter represent opportunities for improving financial literacy and education in that particular area. Appendix A represents some of the Commission's background research into opportunities and challenges surrounding financial education that formed the development of the *National Strategy*.

The Commission took great efforts to include all points of view in the deliberative process, including the following:

First, on August 26, 2004, the Commission issued a notice in the *Federal Register* with a request for comments on the *National Strategy*. In response to that notice, more than 150 comments were received from private citizens, nonprofit organizations, academia, Federal, state, and local agencies, and others.

Second, the Commission conducted six sector-specific public meetings to gather more information from respondents to the August *Federal Register* notice. These meetings were held in various locations in Washington, D.C., between February 25th and March 17th, 2005 Both the *Federal Register* notice and the summaries from the sector-specific meetings are contained in the appendices of the Strategy.

Finally, the Commission convened a working group of 13 Commission agencies to provide significant input into the Strategy, drafted by the Treasury Department. Working group representatives met on eleven separate occasions between June of 2004 and June of 2005 at the Treasury Department to discuss timelines, structure, and content of the document.

Title V, Section 514 of the FACT Act states, in part, that the Strategy "shall provide for participation by state and local governments and private, nonprofit, and public institutions in the creation and implementation of such strategy." This mandate recognizes that both the private sector and the public sector are essential in improving financial literacy in America. In adherence to this mandate, the Strategy examines and discusses financial education resources from the Federal, state, and local governments, and from private sector providers.

The Treasury Department considered a variety of the non-Federal government programs that it learned about in one of the following ways:

a. The programs were cited by a respondent to the *Federal Register* notice on August 26, 2004, which requested public comment on financial education resources for the National Strategy. The comment period closed October 31, 2004. Or,
b. The programs were recommended by organizations in response to outreach by the Treasury Department to promote a broad sampling of programs.

The non-Federal government programs that are discussed in the report were found by the Treasury Department to contain at least six out of the following eight elements, which were developed by the Treasury Department's Office of Financial Education in 2003, in which the program:

1. content focuses on basic savings, credit management, homeownership and/or retirement planning.
2. content is tailored to its target audience, taking into account its language, culture, age, and experience.
3. is offered through a local distribution channel that makes effective use of community resources and contacts.
4. follows up with participants to reinforce the message and ensure that participants are able to apply the skills taught.
5. establishes specific goals and uses performance measures to track progress toward meeting those goals.
6. demonstrates a positive impact on participants' attitudes, knowledge, or behavior through testing, surveys, or other objective evaluation.
7. can be easily replicated on a local, regional, or national basis so as to have broad impact and sustainability.
8. is built to last as evidenced by factors such as continuing financial support, legislative backing, or integration into an established course of instruction.

The purpose of including these non-Federal governmental programs was to give specific, concrete examples of financial education efforts that specifically illustrate the issues discussed in each chapter. The United States Government, including the Financial Literacy and Education Commission and its member agencies, does not endorse the non-Federal governmental entities referenced in this report, nor does it guarantee in any way the services, advice or products provided by non-Federal governmental entities mentioned in this report. eference in this report to any specific financial institution, commercial product, process, or service does not constitute an endorsement, approval, or recommendation by the United States Government, including the Financial Literacy and Education Commission or any of its member agencies, nor does it certify or indicate that non-Federal governmental agencies mentioned in this report—or any of their services, advice or products—are in compliance with or satisfy requirements of, applicable laws or regulations. With regard to the Web site addresses that appear in this report that are created and maintained by non- Federal governmental entities, the United States Government, including the Financial Literacy and Education Commission and its member agencies, does not endorse, approve, certify, or control those external sites and does not guarantee the accuracy, completeness, efficacy, or timeliness of the information contained on these sites.

Moreover, the programs described in the Strategy are, by no means, an exhaustive list of programs that have a positive impact on financial literacy, and are intended to be used for illustrative purposes within the topical chapters.

1. General Saving

Overview

Savings provide the ability to reach important life goals such as financing homeownership and a college education, coping with unexpected events, and preparing for retirement. Even a small amount of savings can grow and compound over time, contributing to the financial security we all seek.

As a nation we have seen a marked decline in personal savings. Thirty-five years ago, 9.4 percent of disposable income was set aside for savings.[1] In 2004, the comparable figure was 1.3 percent.[2] Alan Greenspan, former Chairman of the Board of Governors of the Federal Reserve System, said the following about the importance of personal saving: "A key component of domestic saving in the United States in future decades will be the path of the personal savings rate. That rate will depend on a number of factors, especially the behavior of the members of the baby-boom cohort during their retirement years." [3]

Challenges

While many reasons account for the United States' current personal saving situation, it is clear that, for many Americans, this is a complex issue that requires deep understanding of individual situations and decision-making. For some, the challenge is about the value of personal saving early in life. For others, it requires careful planning. And for still others, it demands a better understanding of the skills and mechanisms needed to save.

Moreover, it is important that Americans have the information, knowledge, and skills to identify their saving goals (e.g., saving for future education expenses, a down payment on a home, retirement, etc.) and then select the instruments and products they can use to help them attain those goals. With increased education on the benefits of saving, Americans can achieve a greater understanding of the importance and benefits of saving, as well as the strategies that support systematic saving and wealth accumulation.

Issues in General Saving

1. Shifting Public Discussion from Consumption to Saving through Public Awareness Campaigns

There is a great deal of competition for a modern family's income. Each month, the average family writes checks for rent or mortgage, childcare, and utilities. Couple those monthly expenses with outlays for transportation, food, clothing, tuition bills for children, student loan payments, and expenses for the care of aging parents, and families are left with limited discretionary income.

When deciding how to allocate discretionary income, families are faced with strong and persuasive messages that encourage them to spend their money. By comparison, families may receive little information and encouragement about saving. Knowing the "how" and "why" of saving can equip Americans with the tools to make wise choices when allocating what often are limited discretionary resources.

Part of building savings is protecting those savings through the use of insurance. When planning their saving and other financial matters, individuals should budget funds to insure their health, home, auto, and life. In this way, Americans can reduce the likelihood that one catastrophic event will wipe out a lifetime of saving.

Through integrated mass-media public awareness efforts, Americans can learn more about the benefits of saving. The issue of saving is a crucial one for all Americans, and public service announcement (PSA) campaigns can help many understand the importance of saving.

By communicating directly with people, using communication channels that have earned their trust and with which they are familiar, and by developing messages that in form, format, and function they are comfortable with, PSA campaigns can educate the nation on the benefits of personal saving and the specific steps each individual and family can and should consider taking. Such PSAs might involve short segments on radio and television, distributing materials via the Web and community-based locations, or hosting other educational activities. These campaigns should be ongoing, providing the public with information and follow-up over time.

Across the nation, there are individual programs, both private and public, using PSA campaigns focused on the topic of saving.

National PSA Multi-Media Campaign

One national PSA campaign uses the full spectrum of media across the nation — including television, radio, print, the Web, transit rail and bus ads, conferences, and more to carry the message of saving. The campaign is designed to focus public attention on what is needed to achieve financial security and promotes the idea that saving today is vital to a secure financial tomorrow. Since 1997, the campaign has secured more than $20 million worth of donated airtime to broadcast the PSAs.

The program is just one part of this organization's efforts to raise public awareness on the actions individuals need to take to facilitate their long-term personal financial independence. This not-for-profit national coalition of public- and private-sector institutions works through its partners to educate Americans on all aspects of personal finance and wealth development, including credit management, college saving, home purchases, and retirement planning.

Local/National PSA Campaign and Saving Program

While traditionally PSA campaigns provide information to the public, some PSA campaigns prompt individuals to take action and get involved. For instance, in 2001 the citizens of an Ohio city were initially targeted by a local public awareness campaign that encouraged and assisted less affluent Americans to save and build wealth. Now the saving campaign reaches a national audience and includes more than 50 local and national initiatives of for-profit, nonprofit, and government organizations that target specific groups, such as African Americans, Hispanic Americans, military personnel, faith- based groups, and young Americans. Not only does the campaign feature public service announcements, but it also delivers information and services to encourage people to enroll as "savers." Each saver must commit to working toward a monetary goal with a specific plan that includes monthly deposits in a specified account. In return, savers receive free information about saving strategies and accounts, a quarterly newsletter, and access to advice from certified financial planners.

These saving public awareness programs are offered and supported by more than 1,000 organizations, including more than 100 financial institutions which are offering no- or low-balance savings accounts to those registered savers. As a result of their efforts, more than 30,000 Americans have enrolled as savers, and hundreds of thousands have sought savings information from the program.

Public Awareness Week on Importance of Insurance

Greater public awareness about the importance of insurance can reduce the likelihood that one catastrophic event will wipe out a lifetime of savings. This national association promotes its annual public awareness week which focuses on how to help consumers avoid fraud in purchasing insurance, review insurance coverage levels, utilize their state's insurance departments, and talk to their insurance providers about possible discounts. In 2004, 45 states and the District of Columbia participated in this public awareness campaign delivered through television and radio, as well as through dedicated phone banks where consumers could ask questions and voice concerns.

In a recent survey, 72 percent of Americans indicated that they have the right amount of insurance coverage, but only 32 percent indicated that they understood the details of those policies "very well." [4]

Thus, the public awareness campaign focuses on meeting this need by giving consumers important information about insurance.

Summary

PSA campaigns represent one method of raising public awareness in ways that help Americans to develop and maintain a saving mindset. Through carefully planned and executed PSA campaigns, the American public can gain a better understanding of the value of saving, the specific steps to take in order to achieve personal saving goals, and the benefits that come from a lifetime of reasonable saving. Public awareness campaigns also can bring together a variety of organizations that target specific groups and offer concrete opportunities for individuals to become savers.

2. Using Existing Tax Incentives to Make Saving More Convenient and Affordable

In decades past, passbooks and piggy banks represented saving plans. Saving money is an activity that requires forethought, planning, specific activities, and responsibility, and is often undertaken without a known, specific "pay off" in the end. While spending is often seen as convenient and affordable, is an exercise in patience and tenacity with a view of achieving — or preparing for — a better future or paving the way to handle unexpected crises or emergencies.

To build wealth, simple lessons about saving are the most important to convey. Even a small amount of savings today can compound into resources for tomorrow. Such resources can provide the financial security and flexibility to handle unexpected events, while simultaneously offering the means for meeting future financial needs and planning.

In their efforts to save more, Americans should use the full spectrum of available savings products and tools. Saving tools are broader than just passbooks and piggy banks. As the public and private sectors continue to innovate to meet the growing and diverse financial needs of the nation, saving can be both convenient and affordable.

Such innovation touches all corners of our day-to-day lives. For instance, Health Savings Accounts (HSAs) and Coverdell Education Savings Accounts (ESAs) empower families to plan and manage their savings for specific health and education expenses anticipated in their future.

Health Savings Accounts

For some consumers, HSAs are innovative programs to encourage personal savings and planning for future healthcare expenses. Modeled after Archer Medical Savings Accounts, HSAs are essentially savings plans to pay for health care costs. These accounts enable tax-free payment for current health expenses while also allowing those enrolled to save for future qualified medical and retiree health expenses. As an Individual Retirement Account (IRA) encourages retirement savings, an HSA encourages health care savings.

Any adult who is covered by a high-deductible health plan (and has no other first-dollar coverage) may establish an HSA.[5] To encourage saving for health expenses after retirement, individuals age 55 and older are allowed to make additional catch-up contributions to their HSAs until they enroll in Medicare.

The money in an HSA is owned and controlled by the individual, and spending decisions do not require the involvement of a health insurer or any other third party. HSA holders decide what types of investments to make with their money, thereby controlling the growth in their HSA accounts. While some companies may establish HSAs for their employees, individuals can sign up for this type of account with banks, credit unions, insurance companies, and other approved companies.

Coverdell Education Savings Accounts

ESAs provide another example of an innovative savings product that was created as an incentive to help parents and students save for education expenses. Parents of students under the age of 18 may contribute up to $2,000 per child per year. The student will not owe tax on the distributions if, for a year, the distributions from an account are not more than a beneficiary's qualified education expenses at an eligible education institution. This benefit applies to higher education expenses as well as to elementary and secondary education expenses.

Generally, any individual (including the beneficiary) can contribute to a Coverdell ESA if the individual's modified adjusted gross income is less than $110,000 ($220,000 if the individual is filing a joint return). The $2,000 maximum contribution per beneficiary is gradually reduced if the contributor's modified adjusted gross income is higher. Distributions are tax-free as long as funds are used for qualified education expenses, such as tuition, books, fees, etc., at an eligible educational institution. An eligible educational institution includes any public, private or religious school that provides elementary or secondary education as determined under state law.

Summary

These examples are just two of the many mechanisms within the tax code that provide incentives for saving for specific future needs. Americans should carefully evaluate these and the multitude of other saving opportunities to determine how best to meet their current and future financial needs.

3. Tailoring Communications to Make Saving Relevant to Everyone

In addition to the broader efforts launched by widely distributed PSA campaigns, there are significant opportunities to utilize targeted programs that address individual audiences or groups of people. By making messages as relevant as possible to the individual, organizers can boost the effectiveness of programs.

To accomplish this, program designers must first determine, through market research, audience financial interests and expectations. From this data, program organizers can begin identifying the appropriate classes, materials, and knowledgeable experts (e.g., financial planners, bankers, etc.) to deliver information on saving to the specific audience. Program designers also should use this process to ensure that particular financial needs and demands are addressed, while maintaining sensitivity to issues such as native language, Internet access, and other communications challenges.

Saving means different things to different people. Tailored education efforts, such as those undertaken by the USDA and DoD, can maximize the reach and effectiveness of general saving activities.

United States Department of Agriculture Cooperative State Research, Education, and Extension Service

Rural Americans face many of the same challenges as those in non-rural areas, such as excessive credit card debt, poor financial planning, lack of savings for retirement and absence of skills for navigating a complex financial marketplace. Unfortunately, due to distance and lack of services (including educational opportunities), rural residents may not have the same resources as those living in urban places. That is why organizations such as the Cooperative Extension System, working in partnership with the USDA CSREES, reaches out to rural Americans, in addition to those in more populated areas, with workshops, home-study courses, Internet-based curricula and other educational methods.

To help individuals focus on their longterm financial situations, for instance, the Cooperative Extension System established its *Financial Security in Later Life* initiative.

Through a package of Web-based and face-to-face programs, the effort encourages participants to plan for retirement and potential long-term health care costs, act to save and invest, and evaluate their own financial conduct to ensure that their actions are on track to to achieve their financial goals.

As of January 2005, 24 states reported 36,563 individuals enrolled in one or more of the *Financial Security in Later Life's* eight educational program curricula.[6] As a result, 90 percent of participants increased financial knowledge, 62 percent planned to use recommended financial planning practices, and 48 percent planned to manage their use of credit, reduce debt, and/or reduce household spending.[7] A group of 7,574 individuals who completed programs report a total of $6,307,708 of annual financial impact, such as dollars saved, debt reduced, or new dollars invested.[8]

Military Saves

For those serving in the U.S. military, saving presents a unique challenge, particularly for junior-level enlisted individuals between the ages of 18 and 21. Nearly a quarter (24 percent) of enlisted servicemen and women do not save at all and almost half only save what is remaining after monthly expenses, meaning they have no systematic saving plans in place. That is why the DoD is developing specific saving programs tailored especially for service personnel who need to begin saving to prepare for their futures.

Based on a model of a consumer organization's campaign, pilots of this social marketing effort have demonstrated the same level of success in motivating service members to reduce debt and establish savings for the future. Some of the pilot locations have proven the *Military Saves* campaign can motivate service members to take action. At one location, 50 percent of the audience signed up, agreeing to save $93,000 in the first year of saving.

Summary

Encouraging individuals to save is an effective message only if it reaches those whom it is intended to help. Accordingly, it is critical that awareness and education efforts ensure that all materials and activities are translated into appropriate languages as needed and targeted to address the interests of a wide range of ages, geographic communities, and economic levels. By tailoring messages and activities to those who need it, organizations can ensure that messages not only reach but also resonate with target audiences.

A greater emphasis should be placed on tailoring communications and education programs specifically to various age groups, demographics, and audiences. The goal is to use a multitude of messages and approaches so that each message received is relevant to the targeted individuals and groups.

Calls to Action

Tactics Employed: Public Awareness, Targeting

1-1 In the first quarter of 2006, the Treasury Department will partner with a nonprofit organization to develop and implement a public service announcement on the benefits of lifetime savings and the savings resources available on the Financial Literacy and Education Commission's Web site, MyMoney.gov.

1-2 Organizations advocating for increased saving should augment their general communication approach with customized messages to address the interests of members of specific age groups, geographic communities, and economic levels.

2. Homeownership

Overview

In 2001, President George W. Bush said "...homeownership lies at the heart of the American Dream. It is a key to upward mobility for low- and middle-income Americans. It is an anchor for families and a source of stability for communities. It serves as the foundation of many people's financial security. And it is a source of pride for people who have worked hard to provide for their families." [9]

To households, communities, and the nation at large, homeownership conveys significant economic and social benefits. Accordingly, for more than 70 years, homeownership has long been an important public policy goal[10] promoted by the Federal government and the focus of key policies and programs.

In 2004, 69 percent of American households owned their own homes — an all-time high. Homeownership is important to all Americans because it represents a significant asset for households. In 2001, 97 percent of all homeowners held at least some equity in their homes, with a median national equity value of $70,000. Home equity represented 42 percent of their net worth.[11]

Homeownership also can be one of the most effective means for low- and moderate-income families to build wealth. For moderate-income homeowners, home equity represents 60 percent of net worth; and for low-income homeowners, it is 80 percent of net worth.[12] In fact, while the net worth of a typical low-income household is $7,900, it is more than six times that, $50,000, for moderate income homeowners.[13]

Challenges

Despite the benefits that can accrue from owning a home, for a multitude of reasons, homeownership may not be in the financial best interest of some families. However, for those positioned for homeownership, it represents an important financial milestone and should be accessible to consumers for whom ownership is financially beneficial. Some Americans may view owning their own homes as a challenge for various reasons, including negative credit histories, daunting down payments and closing cost requirements, and complex loan transactions. For some, basic homebuyer education or promotion of specialized loan products may be all that is needed to help move them toward homeownership. For others, intensive, long-term counseling and credit repair may be necessary.

Technology and innovation have resulted in the creation of a plethora of mortgage loan products that are complex and possess features that may be inappropriate, very risky, and financially detrimental for some consumers, such as adjustable rate mortgages and interest-only loans where payment levels can change dramatically over the term of the loan. In today's highly complicated and technical mortgage market, the greatest challenge to consumers is to be equipped to evaluate the vast array of products and identify those that are most beneficial to their individual circumstances and financial well-being.

Further, as the mortgage lending market has become more competitive and prolific, the emergence of unscrupulous lenders has created concern regarding predatory lending practices Through aggressive marketing tactics, misrepresentation, and fraud, such creditors strip equity from homeowners by entangling them in mortgages with terms that are disadvantageous to the homeowner. In some communities, such lending has led to very high rates of foreclosure and has resulted in financial ruin for homeowners victimized by predatory lenders. While some regulatory and legislative interventions have been undertaken to thwart predatory lending, financial education is viewed as a critical component of protecting homeowner equity.

Community-based programs can be effective in both promoting and preserving homeownership. Local homeownership initiatives can raise awareness and move many individuals and families closer to making the dream of homeownership a reality. Similarly, intervention at a community level for homeowners in financial difficulty can help mitigate the effect of predatory lending for consumers and communities.

Issues in Homeownership

1. Using Grassroots Approaches to Deliver Counseling and Training Programs

Currently, homeownership counseling and training programs address specific stages of homeownership — pre-purchase, post-purchase, equity extraction, and foreclosure mitigation To successfully educate consumers on these issues, curricula should move beyond this model and be responsive to the financial circumstances of borrowers and owners at all stages. Successful programs also need to address a range of other challenges, including language and cultural issues, and geographic impediments in rural communities. There is no "one-sizefits-all" solution to explaining how to achieve and maintain homeownership.

Many local or grassroots organizations are well-positioned to deliver homebuying information and counseling because of their familiarity with the local market. National non-profit organizations, financial institutions, including credit unions, and housing partnerships, offer a variety of information and personal counseling to potential homebuyers. Moreover, Federal efforts through the HUD's Local Homeownership Centers also help families realize the potential benefits of homeownership and assist them in the home mortgage process.

NeighborWorks America® uses Grassroots Network to Provide Counseling

Many Americans turn to non-profit organizations to receive homebuying counseling and training that specifically target their local communities.[14] *NeighborWorks America®* is a national non-profit organization comprised of more than 230 resident-led, chartered groups operating within a larger nationwide coalition of local non-profit partnerships of residents, business leaders, and public officials.

This Congressionally chartered, Federally funded, nonprofit organization uses a variety of methods to increase support for low-income families' access to homeownership, which includes personal counseling, homeownership centers, and partnerships with lending organizations. The organization has established the nation's largest force of certified homeownership education counselors and has provided counseling to more than 471,000 individuals. It has also supported the development of 78 Homeownership Centers throughout the nation. The Centers, created in 1997, are one-stop shops for a broad range of homeownership services available to low- and moderate-income families. The organization also seeks to cultivate partnerships with the government and the private sector to provide affordable loans to potential homebuyers, and has established a national foreclosure prevention center to help address issues related to unscrupulous and predatory lending practices and to identify and prevent foreclosure for current homeowners.

A *NeighborWorks America®* organization in Chicago has collaborated with city officials and more than 20 lenders to reduce geographically concentrated foreclosures through its homeownership preservation initiative. Through innovative outreach, intensive counseling and intervention, and a targeted public awareness campaign, this organization prevented 650 foreclosures in an 18-month period. *NeighborWorks America®* is currently undertaking efforts to replicate this initiative in Ohio and in other communities beset by high foreclosure rates.

Local Credit Union offers First Time Homebuyer Program

For decades, financial institutions, including credit unions across the nation, have successfully delivered community-specific counseling and training to their members, meeting the specific financial needs of the individuals and communities they were established to serve. In return, prospective homebuyers have turned to credit unions to help them navigate the homebuying process and provide the services they need to achieve homeownership.

For instance, one such credit union in Maryland offers members a first- time homebuyer program that provides step-by-step assistance through the homebuying process. To complement this program, the credit union provides a series of online self-help classes entitled *Fundamentals of Personal Finance: Making Informed Choices* and ongoing educational workshops and seminars, such as renting versus buying.

Armed Services Credit Union Serves Military Families

A second example is an armed services credit union which focuses on providing financial services to its unique customer base of more than 2.5 million members worldwide consisting of Navy and Marine Corps personnel and their families. Credit union staff visit their customers on Navy ships, and conduct over 200 general financial presentations annually on the importance of good credit, financial management, credit reports, maintaining good credit, budgeting skills, budgetary counseling, identity theft, and others. The credit union also provides online tools, brochures, and a quarterly member newsletter covering issues such as money management, credit scores, and the factors that contribute to those scores.

Native American Housing Partnership Offers Assistance On or Near Reservation

Public-private housing partnerships bring together non-profit, for-profit, and government sectors in a particular local community to address issues such as affordable housing, financing, and barriers to homeownership. Housing partnerships on Native American reservations are particularly situated to provide information and assistance to often remote areas in a way that seeks to overcome cultural differences. One such housing partnership brings specific grassroots programs and materials directly to the local community on the reservation and at the workplace. It seeks to improve understanding of homeownership issues and access to homeownership, including providing mediation for the buyer with tribal and other governmental authorities and environmental clearances.

Created to provide innovative and flexible homeownership financing opportunities on or near the reservation, the housing partnership empowers Native American families with new knowledge, skills, and understanding to enable families to build, buy, or renovate homes. Through the program, individuals participate in homebuying and financial literacy classes and learn how to establish individual development accounts. Native American families also turn to the housing partnership to make first mortgage financing more accessible and to secure secondary financing through down payments, closing costs, and principal reduction assistance

HUD Local Homeownership Centers

Grassroots organizations also are supported through Federal efforts in HUD's four regional homeownership centers, located in Pennsylvania, Georgia, Colorado, and California. Together, these four centers reach all parts of the country and provide current and prospective homeowners with information not only about the Federal Housing Administration (FHA) and its single-family mortgage insurance programs, but also non-FHA homeownership programs, counseling, mortgage servicing, and other issues relating to homeownership.

Summary

Utilizing grassroots approaches to encourage homeownership, financial institutions and community organizations can empower all Americans to transform the dream of owning a home into a reality. Through face-to-face counseling and targeted education programs, grassroots programs can help families achieve, maintain, and sustain homeownership.

2. Highlighting Success through Quality Education and Public Awareness

Successful education and public awareness programs are only as strong as the messages they deliver and the curriculum and instructors they use. Homebuyer education and awareness programs need to be of the highest quality and should be delivered by qualified instructors who understand the information and know how best to relate it to prospective homebuyers.

The credible homebuying and mortgage education and awareness programs seek to equip potential homebuyers with the knowledge they need to make wise decisions, and are not simply focused on selling a particular product. These programs highlight homeownership success stories, and encourage individuals to connect homeownership with investments and savings. Public awareness efforts, such as those created by a housing partnership in Ohio, deliver clear messages of the benefits of owning your own home, as opposed to renting. Moreover, education efforts, such as those provided by the HUD, certified housing counselors, and *National Homeownership Month* help promote successful savings and homeownership.

Housing Partnership in Ohio

In one city in Ohio, residents are learning how to become successful homeowners and gaining necessary financial skills from the local housing partnership. Basing its efforts on proven successful programs and public education activities, this housing partnership has established a homeownership marketing campaign called *Fire the Landlord Now*. Through colorful, contemporary ads placed in the local transit authority buses, such as "Fire the Landlord Now." "Buy a lot of home for a little green," the housing partnership was able to attract potential low- and middle- income homebuyers to its resources. Phone calls to the housing partnership and the amount of homeownership counseling have dramatically increased.

U.S. Department of Housing and Urban Development

As the primary Federal agency on homebuying, HUD is uniquely positioned to help homeowners and prospective homeowners access quality, effective homebuyer education programs. To this end, HUD provides contact information for homeownership counseling services on a state-by-state, district-by-district basis through a comprehensive Internet resource, www.hud.gov/local/index.cfm. (The HUD Housing Counseling agencies are found at this link: www.hud.gov/ offices/hsg/sfh/hcc/hccprof14.cfm.) States listed on the site feature their local homeownership events and strategies. HUD also operates a toll-free number for consumers to locate a counseling agency in their community. Both the Web site and toll-free number are highlighted in all of HUD's brochures and publications.

HUD created the program *Neighborhood Networks* in 1995 to encourage property owners to establish community technology centers in HUD-insured and assisted properties. Today, more than 1,100 *Neighborhood Networks* centers help to improve the quality of life for residents by: (1) providing job training and placement, (2) creating employment and educational opportunities, (3) advancing literacy and language skills programs, and (4) providing access to healthcare information and other social services. The *Neighborhood Networks'* "Train-the-Trainer" Sessions enable NN center directors to provide resources for multifamily housing residents and their surrounding communities. These individuals are trained in topic areas based on the resident's needs which are identified through surveys of NN center clients.

National Standard for Pre-purchase Homeownership Education and Certification for Counselors and Trainers

The *NeighborWorks America® Campaign for Home Ownership* has set a national standard for pre-purchase homeownership education and established a five-day training and certification course for counselors and trainers. Trainers certified by *NeighborWorks America®* adhere to the following standards:

All potential homebuyers receive a minimum of eight hours of group homebuyer education with follow-up individual counseling;
The housing counselors are certified after completing the five-day "Homebuyer Education Methods: Training-for-Trainers" class and passing the course exam;
The content, delivery and format of the homebuyer training is tailored to meet the needs of the participants (rather than a "one-size-fits-all" approach);
Ideally, the training and counseling occur before a purchase contract is signed;
Customer satisfaction surveys are used to evaluate the effectiveness of the training; and
All volunteer trainers must adhere to a code of ethics.[15]

National Homeownership Month

American consumers are learning about the value of homeownership from leaders at the highest levels, including the President. Since 2002, President George W. Bush has proclaimed the month of June as *National Homeownership Month*, calling on the people of the United States to join him in recognizing the importance of providing all citizens a chance to achieve the American Dream.

During *National Homeownership Month*, Americans are encouraged to learn more about financial management and how to take advantage of the homeownership opportunities available to them in their communities. In 2005, *National Homeownership Month* stressed that the journey to homeownership involves more than simply finding a real estate agent and obtaining a mortgage. *National Homeownership Month* featured a five-city tour which was a collaboration among twelve Federal agencies and showcased the numerous programs available to individuals. Several other homeownership events occurred simultaneously throughout the country during the month of June. These programs focused on teaching the "howtos" of buying a first home. Through this education effort, individuals and families discovered how to become homeowners, an important step in safeguarding their financial futures that also contributes to the overall strength of our nation.

Summary

An increased public awareness of best practices and successes, particularly at the local level, can result in increased understanding and acceptance of homeownership as a foundation for financial security. By linking financial literacy and homeownership, awareness efforts can promote effective strategies on a broader scale. Through expanded public education efforts and an integrated mass media campaign, organizations can expand access to the range of educational resources available to consumers, particularly by promoting best practices and success stories.

3. Community Collaboration Can Be Invaluable in Developing and Distributing Programs

Worthwhile education and training programs are only of value if the individuals they are intended for are aware of their availability and take full advantage of what is offered. For instance, many renters may not know where to obtain information on homeownership or how to get assistance in setting homeownership goals; thus, they need to be exposed to messages that will direct them to the appropriate programs.

Moreover, connecting the right people with the right financial messages can be a challenging task for any one organization to accomplish alone. For instance, one program may have the expertise, but not the on-the-ground presence. By partnering, organizations can pool their resources to achieve common objectives.

Truly successful homeownership awareness initiatives require collaboration among all sectors that target the specific groups that need information the most. By working together, public- and private- sector organizations can demystify the homeownership process and provide consumers with the tools necessary to become homeowners. Organizations, such as a homeownership network in Montana, a housing association in California, and a faith-based housing agency in Michigan, demonstrate how homeownership programs that target specific groups can serve as successful education tools.

Lenders and Government Agencies in Partnership in Montana Provide Counseling and Find Financing for Potential Homebuyers

Public and private sector organizations have joined together to provide Montana residents with the information and access they need to successfully navigate the entire homebuying and homeownership process. Through a system of service delivery partners, the organizations promote homeownership throughout 184 Montana communities. Lenders and government agencies partner to provide financing for down payments and closing cost loans for first-time homebuyers, single heads of households, and families with a disabled member. The organizations also provide residents with homebuyer education, foreclosure prevention counseling, and individual counseling.

Nonprofits and Government Agencies in Partnership in a City in California Provide Housing and Savings Match Program

The government and the private sector have joined together to provide the education, training, and assistance that residents in a Californian city need to make homeownership a reality. The housing association in that city not only develops, owns, and operates affordable multi-family housing, but also seeks to establish strong and stable communities through resident participation and leadership development.

A key focus is to build assets — including both skills and wealth — of residents to ensure long-term self sufficiency.

Toward that end, the housing association established an individual development account program that matches the personal savings of residents with donated funds. As part of financial education classes, participants are required to put aside a small percentage of their earned income into savings accounts attached to a particular asset-building goal (e.g., home purchase), with a savings match — two-dollars matched for each one-dollar saved — from the housing association made possible through private donations. By providing economic literacy training, mentoring, and asset accumulation, the program helps citizens realize their dreams of homeownership.

Housing Counseling Agency Teams with Faith-Based Organization in Michigan to Reach New Clients

Access to financial literacy information has become easier for residents in one Michigan city, thanks to a faith-based housing counseling agency. This housing counseling agency was established as an outreach effort through a local church, and it has counseled approximately 32,000 individuals on homeownership through faith-based and community- based organizations. Approximately 6,000 of those clients have become homeowners with the help of this agency. As part of the HUD National Intermediary for Housing Counseling, this housing counseling agency oversees 23 affiliated faith-based organizations that provide housing counseling services in Michigan communities.

Summary

Homeownership can be a complex process for the average family to understand. Through public-private and private- private collaboration, public awareness and education programs can successfully deliver homebuyer education and counseling efforts. Partnerships between public and private sector organizations can help those individuals and families who are underrepresented in the homeownership market better understand how they can become homeowners

CALLS TO ACTION

Tactic Employed: Partnerships

2-1 Between the second quarter of 2006 and the second quarter of 2007, the U.S. Department of Housing and Urban Development will join with the Treasury Department to host a series of meetings highlighting the work of successful partnerships that have advanced homeownership.

2-2 Lenders and other businesses should partner with grassroots organizations to provide financial education on buying a home and one-on-one counseling to demystify the homebuying process.

3. RETIREMENT SAVING

Overview

Today, the retirement landscape is dramatically different than it was in previous generations. Americans are now living longer than in years past, health care costs represent a much larger proportion of retirement expenses, and workers are expected to take more individual responsibility for their retirement saving due to a shift from traditional defined benefit plans to defined contribution plans. As a result, it is more important than ever that Americans employ lifelong strategies to build retirement saving.

The average life expectancy for those born today is 78 years, almost a full decade longer than the life expectancy of those born in 1950.[16] In 2002, the life expectancy of a 65-year-old individual rose to 83, while a 75-year-old person may live more than 11 additional years.[17] With those 11 years come increased health and living expenses that require planning. While seven in 10 Americans are somewhat confident that they will have enough money to live comfortably in retirement, only 42 percent have actually calculated what they will need and what they need to save to reach their retirement goals.[18]

As the nation grows older and the retirement landscape continues to change, there is more of an impetus to properly plan and save for retirement. Social Security continues to play an important part in Americans' retirement security. In fact, Social Security currently provides 50 percent or more of the income for two- thirds of married couples and unmarried persons (age 65 or older) receiving Social Security benefits, and is the only source of income for 22 percent of such couples and persons.[19] For beneficiaries with average earnings, Social Security retirement benefits will replace only about 40 percent of pre-retirement earnings.

Additionally, the Social Security system itself is facing challenges. With the "baby boom" generation preparing to retire soon, Social Security will be paying out more than it takes in by 2017 and the Social Security trust funds are expected to be exhausted by 2041.[20] At that time, without changes to the program, Social Security will not be able to pay all scheduled benefits. President George W. Bush commented on this situation when he said, "Social Security was a great moral success of the 20th Century, and we must honor its great purposes in this century. The system, however, on its current path, is headed toward bankruptcy. And so we must join together to strengthen and save Social Security."[21] The ongoing public policy discussion on the future of Social Security is something Americans should heed as they make their retirement plans.

Since its inception, Social Security has provided a minimum foundation of protection. A comfortable retirement usually requires not only Social Security, but also personal saving and saving from employer-based plans. In 2001, 64 percent of all wage and salary workers were employed by organizations sponsoring pension plans.[22] While 91 percent of public-sector employees had access to a retirement plan at work, only 60 percent of private-sector employees did.[23] In 2004, only 53.4 percent of all full-time employees participated in an employer-sponsored retirement plan.[24]

Such opportunities to save for retirement are more likely to be found in large firms. Employees of firms with over 100 employees are twice as likely as employees of firms with 100 or fewer employees to have access to and also to participate in a retirement plan.[25] In 2003, 42 percent of workers in small businesses (1-99 employees) had access to retirement plans and 35 percent participated, as opposed to 75 percent and 65 percent respectively of employees in larger firms.[26]

A recent study examined the saving and investing activity of more than 600 employees at a major company considered as "low savers" — those who do not contribute enough to the plan to receive the full company match or do not contribute to the plan at all. The study found that 72 percent didn't know how much they needed to save for retirement, but thought that they should be saving two-to-three times more. Despite this, 77 percent said that they would continue to contribute at their current level and 34 percent said they still did not plan to participate in the plan. The study also identified several barriers to saving, including lack of basic knowledge about their employer's plan, discomfort with investing, procrastination, and debt.[27]

Finally, Americans should consider tax-preferred individual accounts to save for retirement, such as traditional Individual Retirement Accounts (IRA) and Roth IRAs. Approximately 5.7 million American taxpayers contributed to an IRA in 2000, while 6.8 million contributed to a Roth IRA.[28]

Challenges

There are many retirement saving challenges. These include: that life expectancy is increasing; that Social Security alone was not meant to and will not provide an adequate retirement income; that many employees do not have access to employer-sponsored pension plans and many of those who do are not participating; and that many Americans have not even calculated what they will need to save for a comfortable retirement.

As average life expectancy increases and employees are expected to assume greater individual responsibility to prepare and save for retirement, there is a growing need for increased public awareness of the importance of saving for retirement and the ways consumers can seek to achieve that goal. It is important to determine how to best reach and educate those groups of individuals who are not saving adequately and to develop products or campaigns targeted to encourage greater saving. There are specific roles that both large and small employers, as well as government and non-profit organizations, can play to boost understanding of retirement planning and increase employee participation in savings options.

While the challenges are significant, they can be overcome by maximizing available opportunities and providing the educational programs and guidance that have been proven effective in practice.

Financing one's retirement is a complex task, and it requires thorough planning and understanding of the options.

The current discussion on Social Security, initiated by President Bush, has raised awareness about the issue of retirement security and the need to plan for the future. Individuals across the country are engaging in discussions about Social Security, personal retirement accounts, and retirement planning. As more and more people come to understand the real problems facing Social Security, they also understand the need to take action to strengthen the system for future generations.

For effective retirement planning, Americans should focus on the roles that Social Security, employment-based retirement saving, and individual saving will play in their retirement saving.

Issues in Retirement Saving

1. Educating Workers on All Retirement Savings Opportunities

Millions of the Americans in the baby boomer generation will begin to retire between now and 2019. Yet only 62 percent of American workers are saving for retirement.[29] Moreover, only four in 10 workers have taken the time and effort to complete a retirement needs calculation, which is considered the basic planning step designed to help individuals determine how much money they are likely to need in retirement.[30]

As retirement saving options continue to grow, employees need to understand that retirement planning involves more than just paying into the Social Security system. While a minimum foundation and a valuable component of retirement, Social Security is but one of many components of retirement income. Moreover, some employees who have not previously saved for retirement now have the opportunity to make "catch up" contributions to their retirement plans.

Many Federal government agencies are partnering to improve public utilization of available retirement strategies and saving vehicles. The collective goal of these agency efforts is to ensure that Americans are aware of all of the retirement saving options available to them and are equipped to utilize these options in an effective way to improve their overall retirement security.

A wide range of Federal initiatives exist to increase public knowledge of retirement saving while encouraging more Americans to save for retirement. Among such initiatives are specific actions such as the annual distribution of the Social Security Statement, the *National Summit on Retirement Savings (Saver Summit)*, and recent legislative and administrative changes to Federal retirement laws.

Social Security Statement

The SSA is committed to educating all Americans on their individual retirement futures by increasing public understanding of the basic features of Social Security and assisting workers in preparing for their long-term economic security. Through its annual mailing of the Social Security Statement, SSA provides more than 140 million workers over the age of 25 with an earnings summary and estimates of future Social Security retirement benefits, explaining to all Americans the role Social Security can play in a worker's retirement. This statement allows individuals to know whether they have accumulated enough "work credits" to qualify for benefits and, if so, how much those benefits might be.

The Social Security Statement represents one of the Federal government's largest efforts to communicate directly with Americans about Social Security and the need for individuals to prepare in advance for retirement. However, many Americans are not using the information to the fullest extent possible. In fact, a recent Government Accountability Office (GAO) survey indicates that only 66 percent of respondents remember receiving the statement.[31] To expand its educational reach on retirement, SSA supplements the information available on the statement with benefit calculators available at www.socialsecurity.gov/planners and with the wealth of information available at www.socialsecurity.gov and MyMoney.gov.

U.S. Department of Labor – National Summit on Retirement Savings

In the spring of 2006, the DOL will convene its third *Saver Summit*. The purpose of the *Saver Summit* is to advance the public's knowledge of retirement saving and its critical importance to the future well-being of workers and families. The *Saver Summit* will facilitate the development of broad-based public education programs that (1) encourage and enhance individual commitment to a personal retirement saving strategy; (2) identify the problems workers have in setting aside adequate saving for retirement; (3) identify the barriers which employers, especially small employers, face in assisting their workers in accumulating retirement saving; and (4) examine the impact and effectiveness of individual employers to promote personal saving for retirement among their workers and to promote participation in company savings options.

Legislative and Administrative Changes

Specific legislative and administrative efforts have equipped Americans with additional options to properly plan and actively save for retirement. While public education efforts continue to spotlight these positive retirement saving changes, many Americans remain unaware of these changes or do not know where and how to access relevant information. Some examples of these legislative and administrative changes are the ability to make "catch-up" contributions to retirement plans, the DOL Advisory Opinion on providing financial education in the workplace, and the *Saver's Credit*.

In recent years, the Federal government has promoted policy changes that now allow workers to build greater retirement savings, allow older workers to make "catch-up" contributions, and provide incentives to employers to offer retirement plans. The Economic Growth and Tax Relief and Reconciliation Act of 2001 (P.L. 107-16) allows individuals over the age of 50 to make "catch-up" contributions to their retirement saving plans while increasing IRA contribution limits from $2,000 to $4,500.

To encourage employers to provide assistance to their employees, the DOL has provided guidance concerning how employers may safely provide investment advice to defined contribution plan participants in Advisory Opinion 2001-09A.[32] Before this opinion was published, many employers were hesitant to provide certain financial education materials or tools (such as computer programs) to their employees because of concerns regarding liability for providing investment advice.

Finally, the *Saver's Credit*, enacted in 2001, offers specific incentives for low-income workers to save toward retirement. The *Saver's Credit* provides a government matching contribution, in the form of a nonrefundable tax credit, for voluntary individual contributions to 401(k) type plans, IRAs, and similar retirement saving arrangements.

Summary

Efforts are underway across the nation to increase public awareness of the most effective ways to plan and save for retirement. These initiatives attempt to educate Americans on the advantages of various saving products and on new options for retirement saving. Further education efforts aimed at increasing the public's understanding of retirement saving should receive priority attention.

Vehicles for increasing knowledge about and boosting retirement saving include the Social Security Benefits Statement, *Saver Summits*, and legislative and administrative measures. All Americans — young, old, and those in between — should be aware of their Social Security benefits and should read and understand their Social Security Statement. This statement is an effective tool for retirement planning that provides all Americans with a snapshot of what they might expect during their retirement years from the Social Security system. Government agencies, financial organizations, nonprofit organizations and community-based organizations offer a wealth of information intended to help inform individuals about saving for retirement. Current efforts to educate Americans on preparing for retirement should be supplemented with information from other sources, including information that focuses on types of retirement saving vehicles and "catch-up" contributions.

2. Encouraging Retirement Saving for Employees of Large Firms

With the increasing popularity of defined contribution plans, employers are finding that their employees need more assistance in planning for their financial futures. Many employees look to their employers for guidance on whether to save for retirement, how to do it, and how to plan for the future. Employers are frequently viewed as a primary educational resource for reliable information on investment choices, asset allocation strategies, and basic retirement planning.

Many employers meet this employee expectation and provide extensive financial education programs in the workplace to improve retirement saving. In fact, some employers have been able to increase retirement plan participation rates by establishing retirement plans that automatically enroll workers, allowing them to opt-out of retirement saving instead of requiring them to opt in.[33]

Private employers, the Federal government, and nonprofit organizations are all playing roles in distributing information on retirement to employees and in providing a foundation of understanding for all retirement savers. Some private employers are also turning to innovative retirement savings plan features such as automatic enrollment to help employees prepare for the future.

Retirement Education Efforts – Private-Sector Employers

The private sector has demonstrated success in retirement saving education, equipping employees with valued information and services. One such employer provides its workers with a core financial education curriculum. The curriculum includes instructor-led workshops, firm- specific financial education software, a financial counseling help line staffed by financial planners and educators, and access to an online financial campus. This initiative has resulted in both increased 401(k) participation and increased contribution rates.[34]

Another such employer has been offering similar educational programs centered on financial literacy training to its employees for many years. This firm strongly believes that education is a necessary component for integrating employer benefits with employee lives. Employees attend employer-sponsored programs such as *Life Planning 101, Investing in Your Future, and Healthy, Wealthy, and Wise* during work hours. Internal evaluation surveys have demonstrated that these programs regularly receive favorable scores.[35]

Retirement Education Efforts – Federal Government as an Employer

As one of the nation's largest employers, the Federal government engages in a wide range of education activities to prepare its workers for retirement and to encourage retirement saving. Administered by the Federal Retirement Thrift Investment Board (FRTIB), the Thrift Savings Plan (TSP) provides a defined contribution retirement system to Federal civilian employees, Postal employees, and members of the Uniformed Services. To encourage saving, briefings and DVDs are made available for employees. Additionally, agency officials tasked with administering the TSP receive specialized training so they can effectively respond to questions.

The TSP is a tax-deferred defined contribution plan similar to a private- sector 401(k) plan. Generally, all Federal employees hired after 1983 are covered by the Federal Employees Retirement System and are automatically enrolled in the TSP whether or not a salary contribution is made. By law, all Federal agencies contribute an amount equal to one percent of an employee's basic pay into his/her account each pay period. All employee contributions are voluntary with the employing agency matching dollar to dollar the first three percent of pay an employee contributes each pay period, and 50 cents on the dollar for the next two percent of pay. Employees under the older Civil Service Retirement System (CSRS) may contribute to the TSP without any agency match.

Through the Web site www.tsp.gov, employees can access their accounts, use various saving calculators, view online statements, and print account-related forms. FRTIB also provides a toll-free telephone line for participants and their beneficiaries, conducts a communications effort tied to new lifecycle funds, and participates in the OPM-sponsored financial fairs for Federal employees.

Beyond providing the TSP to its employees the Federal government is also attempting to educate the Federal workforce on the need for retirement saving and investment. As part of this effort, OPM has developed a retirement financial literacy and education strategy for employees. This effort provides workers with information on how to plan for retirement and calculate the retirement investment needed to meet individual retirement goals.

The OPM Federal employee retirement strategy is built on the belief that employers need to educate employees about employer-provided benefits while providing resources and guidance on how best to use other programs and efforts to achieve successful retirement. To guide this educational process, OPM surveyed the Federal workforce and is developing a retirement readiness index that will help employees and employers better understand retirement education needs by benchmarking workforce retirement readiness. This approach could serve as a model, educating employers on issues to emphasize retirement saving education to employees.

Retirement Education Efforts – Assistance from Non-profit Organizations

Large employers are also working with non-profit organizations to improve the retirement education being provided to employees. Through various initiatives nonprofit organizations have demonstrated how they can assist large private employers and the Federal government in providing employees with the financial education they need to plan for retirement.

Savings Fitness provides individuals with key information about saving for retirement, and was developed through a partnership between the DOL's Employee Benefits Security Administration and a professional organization of financial service providers. This publication has been featured in leading national media and is distributed through retirement planning workshops and through the Commission's Web site, MyMoney.gov.

Also, a professional organization of certified public accountants developed a multi-faceted program which included lessons on retirement. This effort takes a broad leadership role in educating the American public — from school children to retirees and those in between — on financial topics that apply specifically to each age group's particular stage of life. Retirement saving efforts focus on annuities and retirement planning, borrowing or withdrawing money from a 401(k), closing a retirement income gap, estimating retirement income needs, and understanding defined benefit plans, among others.

Retirement Plan Feature Options – Automatic Enrollment Plans

To help their employees maximize retirement opportunities and effectively save for their futures, some large employers are implementing automatic 401(k) enrollment plans. Under automatic enrollment plans, employees are automatically enrolled in the retirement saving program unless they actively choose not to participate.

Automatic enrollment plans differ from the traditional 401(k) plans that require workers to actively choose to participate in the TSP. Under the traditional opt- in structure of most

401(k) plans, many workers never choose to save in the first place, thereby, losing out on a sound saving and investment opportunity. Additionally, many employees forfeit the opportunity to receive a company match if they fail to contribute to their 401(k) plans. Automatic enrollment encourages active involvement of employees.

With automatic enrollment, employee contributions, which increase gradually over time, are invested prudently and preserved for retirement, all without putting the onus on workers to take the initiative for any of these steps. Workers remain free to override the default options – choosing whether to save or not to save and controlling how their savings are invested – but those who fail to exercise their retirement saving are not left out.

The effects of automatic enrollment are distinctly positive, with studies showing that automatic enrollment increases both participation in 401(k) plans and the level of employee contributions.[36] Automatic enrollment features are used by a number of large U.S. firms.

Summary

Employer-based financial education has proven effective in helping workers plan and save for retirement.[37] By establishing their own retirement education programs and materials or partnering with non-profit education efforts, employers can help their employees understand their retirement plans and assist employees in planning and saving appropriately for the future. Specific emphasis should be placed on helping large employers institute innovative retirement plan features, such as automatic enrollment in 401(k) plans, to increase participation rates and retirement saving.

3. Retirement Saving Options for Employees of Small Businesses

Many small business owners find that they are not familiar with the different retirement plans that are available to them, including the options specifically created for small businesses and designed to be less costly and easy to administer.[38]

For example, 73 percent of small business owners have never heard of or are not very familiar with the Simplified Employee Pension (SEP) and 52 percent have never heard of or are not very familiar with the Savings Incentive Match Plan for Employees of Small Employers (SIMPLE) – two plans that are specifically designed for small businesses.[39] In stark contrast, 85 percent of small business owners are somewhat or very familiar with 401(k) plans, which are designed for employers of all sizes, not specifically for small business owners.[40]

The same range of communications and education activities available to large firms that have the capacity to boost employee understanding of retirement saving also are available to small businesses. Additionally, specific resources are available to small businesses for use in educating small-firm employees on retirement planning.

The DOL provides small business owners and their employees with education resources on retirement plan options, plan management, and employer responsibilities for operating retirement plans.

Retirement Plan Options and Management

To encourage growth in the number of retirement plans available, DOL, in partnership with a national association of business leaders, developed an interactive Web site to help small business employers determine the best plan option for their businesses. This program provides small businesses with information focusing on reasons to offer retirement plans to employees, considerations if a small business does not offer retirement plans, and how plans benefit both employees and the business itself.

To augment this site, DOL partnered with the IRS to develop publications about various types of plans such as SEPs, and SIMPLEs.[41] DOL also offers a series of seminars in conjunction with the IRS and a coalition of business and professional associations to assist small employers in setting up and operating their plans and to educate small business owners about their responsibilities as fiduciaries.

Summary

Helping employees better understand and prepare for retirement is not simply a task for large employers and the Federal government. Small business owners can take advantage of the tools above to offer retirement plans to their workers and can play an important role in encouraging and educating their workers on retirement planning.

4. Taking Advantage of Tax-Preferred Individual Retirement Savings Products

Many Americans do not make full use of tax-preferred retirement saving vehicles, such as the traditional IRA and the Roth IRA. Approximately 5.7 million American taxpayers contributed to an IRA in 2000, while 6.8 million contributed to a Roth IRA.[42] There are many benefits to saving for retirement in these individual accounts, including tax-deductible contributions and tax-free accumulations of investment earnings. With IRAs and Roth IRAs, for instance, families may plan and manage their retirement saving more wisely based on their future needs.

Individual Retirement Accounts (IRA) and Roth IRAs

A traditional IRA is a personal savings account that offers tax advantages to set aside funds for retirement. Annual contributions of up to $4,000 for individuals under age 50 and $4,500 for individuals age 50 or older (in 2005) are fully tax-deductible for workers not covered under employer-sponsored pensions. If an employee is covered by an employer-sponsored pension plan, that employee's deduction for contributions to an IRA is reduced or phased out in accordance with the employee's modified adjusted gross income. Investment earnings for all traditional IRA contributions accumulate tax-free and are not taxed until funds are distributed, usually at a lower tax rate in retirement. Withdrawls from traditional IRAs, made before age 59½, are taxed an additional 10 percent.

In addition, the Taxpayer Relief Act of 1997 created Roth IRAs, which differ from traditional IRAs in that contributions are made with after-tax dollars but earnings and distributions are tax-free. The contribution limit to a Roth IRA in 2005 is $4,000 for individuals under age 50 and $4,500 for individuals age 50 or older. However, as with traditional IRAs, an individual's contribution limit may be reduced or phased out in accordance with his or her modified adjusted gross income. Withdrawls from Roth IRAs, made before age 59½, are taxed an additional 10 percent.

Summary

IRAs and Roth IRAs provide an opportunity for individuals to save for retirement and supplement Social Security benefits and employer-provided pensions. Eligible Americans should be encouraged to use IRAs and Roth IRAs to accumulate retirement savings.

CALLS TO ACTION

Tactics Employed: Targeting, Integration/Teachable Moment

3-1 In 2006, the Treasury Department and the Department of Labor will co-host a roundtable with large employers on retirement saving. Topics will include successful strategies integrating the delivery of financial education into the workplace and other options for increasing participation and contributions in private pensions, such as automatic enrollment.

3-2 The Small Business Administration (SBA), the Department of Labor, and the Treasury Department are committed to conducting outreach to small businesses, and will continue to offer valuable resources on retirement options to small firms. The SBA will make available specific information for small businesses on general retirement issues by providing an online training link that will be available on MyMoney.gov by the second quarter of 2006.

4. CREDIT

Overview

Across the nation, consumers are dealing with increased levels of debt. From January 2003 to January 2005, consumer debt levels increased nine percent, as revolving debt, most typically credit card debt, increased by eight percent, and non revolving debt increased by 10 percent.[43]

This rise in consumer debt is consistent with the increased availability of credit from a variety of lenders. The increase in availability of credit has been fueled in part by technology, which has allowed increased efficiency in credit underwriting and pricing. Technology has significantly increased the ability of creditors to assimilate and process information to make credit risk evaluations and price according to the risk that each applicant represents. This technology also has played an important role in the growth in subprime lending, where creditors extend loans to riskier borrowers at higher rates.

Moreover, between September 2003 and September 2004, there were 1.6 million non-business bankruptcies filed.[44] Providing assistance to those in bankruptcy and other financially troubled consumers has become a growth industry.[45] In terms of the effects of counseling, those seeking reputable financial counseling fare better than those who have not obtained this information. The use of reputable credit counseling has a significant impact on making borrowers more credit worthy, increasing the number of accounts that are paid off, and decreasing total individual debt.[47]

Two important components of consumer credit are credit reports and credit scores. Credit reports contain the historical performance of a consumer's repayment history of financial obligations, including debt contracts, taxes, and utilities. Lenders use this history of performance to assess the repayment risk that a consumer represents. A credit score is the numeric assignment of risk calculated from an algorithm that uses credit report information to predict the likelihood of repayment.

The findings of a recently released GAO report entitled, *Credit Reporting Literacy: Consumers Understood the Basics but Could Benefit from Targeted Educational Efforts*, show that a large percentage of American consumers have a good understanding of the basics of credit reporting: they appear to know how credit reports are used, what information is contained in a credit report, and are aware of their right to dispute inaccurate information.[48] However, many consumers did not appear to understand that credit reports are used to price and underwrite insurance policies and can impact employment.[49] Also, consumers are unaware that they can file a complaint with the FTC if they have found inaccuracies in their credit reports and are dissatisfied with the credit reporting agencies' resolution of the complaint. According to the report, most consumers know what a credit score is, but do not know that some behaviors negatively affect their score.

By better understanding their credit reports, consumers can better manage their financial matters in a way that will help their credit scores. Additionally, consumers who review and understand their credit reports can more easily spot inaccuracies and instances of identity theft.

Challenges

American consumers, regardless of their income level or credit histories, are regularly confronted with numerous credit offers from a wide variety of lenders. As consumer credit increases in the United States, Americans are faced with a variety of issues in making credit decisions. To begin it is important that consumers understand the impact that excessive credit can have on their long-term financial health. Moreover, an understanding of credit scoring and the effects a negative credit history can have on the cost of credit are critically important for consumers in evaluating credit offers.[50] In addition, when Americans choose to obtain credit, it is critically important for them to have an understanding of the terms of credit that are being offered to them so that they can select the credit terms best for them. These challenges are further compounded by not knowing where to seek out specific information and guidance on general credit issues.[51]

Effective educational programs and materials provided by the Federal government, private sector, and nonprofit organizations can help overcome these challenges and equip consumers with knowledge about the costs and benefits of credit, and provide ready access to resources on evaluating credit offers and understanding consumer rights and protections. As consumers are met with aggressive marketing campaigns by creditors on a regular basis and gain increased access to credit, the need to strengthen consumer credit literacy becomes e.g., increasingly important.

Issues in Credit

1. Increasing Public Understanding of Credit, Credit Reports, and Credit Scores

One of the greatest financial challenges American consumers face is gaining access to information, education, and counseling when it is needed most. During critical teachable moments in consumers' lives Americans are in need of guidance and information on personal credit.

Consumer credit education efforts should make consumers aware of their rights under the Fair Credit Reporting Act (FCRA) which allows them to review their credit reports for accuracy. If an error is found or if an item is incomplete, individuals should immediately contact the credit reporting agency that issued the report to have it corrected. The law mandates that the credit reporting agency and the organization that provided the information (such as a bank or credit card company) have the responsibility for correcting inaccurate or incomplete information on individual consumer credit reports. After a consumer inquiry, the credit reporting agency must provide written results to the individual, as well as another free, updated copy of the credit report to the individual if the dispute results in a change. If no change is made, the statement of the dispute will still be included in the official file.

The world of consumer credit transactions can be very complicated. In an effort to increase public understanding of credit, credit reports, and credit scores, public awareness efforts should focus on explaining the fundamental components of credit, such as key terminology (annual percentage rates, principal, interest and finance charges, points and fees, minimum payment, repayment schedules, installments, balloon payments, deferred interest, interest only, etc.), the calculation of finance charges, and the types of credit available (e.g., unsecured credit such as credit cards, overdraft lines of credit, consumer loans, and student loans versus secured credit such as mortgage loans, home equity loans, and home equity lines of credit). High-quality programs also will educate consumers about the providers of credit, including banks, credit unions, thrifts, merchants, and payday lenders.

Consumers throughout the nation have been able to learn about key terminology and parties involved in credit through a wide range of public education initiatives, including the FCRA and the New Free Credit Report Rule, and public resources, such as the new Federal publication, *Your Access to Free Credit Reports*. In addition to Federal sources of guidance, providers of credit, such as credit unions and banks, are making consumers aware of the role of credit and individual credit options. These lender programs include seminars and public campaigns on key topics, such as issues that affect credit scores.

Fair Credit Reporting Act and the New Free Credit Report Rule

The FCRA promotes the accuracy, fairness, and privacy of information in the files of credit reporting agencies. A 2003 amendment to the FCRA, the FACT Act, requires each of the nationwide credit reporting agencies to provide consumers with a free copy of their credit report, upon request, once every 12 months, from www.annualcreditreport.com.[52] Consumers who order a copy of their report online by visiting this Web site should be able to access it immediately. Consumers may also complete and mail the form, the Annual Credit Report Request Form, which is available on the Web site. If the consumer orders the report by calling the toll-free 1-877-322-8228 number, the report will be processed and mailed within 15 days.

A credit report contains information on where a person lives, how a person pays his or her bills, and whether the person has been sued, arrested, or has filed for bankruptcy. Nationwide credit reporting agencies sell the information to creditors, insurers, employers, and other businesses that use it to evaluate applications for credit, insurance, employment, or renting.

Moreover, the FCRA provides additional consumer rights with respect to credit. For example, under this law most consumers have the right to be told about information that is used against them, to ask for a credit score, and to dispute incomplete or inaccurate information.

The law also places responsibilities on the credit reporting agencies. For instance, credit reporting agencies must delete or correct inaccurate or unverifiable information; may not report outdated negative information; and must get consumer consent before providing any information to potential employers.

Federal Trade Commission Publication – Your Access to Free Credit Reports

The FTC has prepared a brochure entitled *Your Access to Free Credit Reports*, available at MyMoney.gov as well as at the FTC's Credit Web site, www.ftc.gov/credit. The brochure describes how to order a free annual credit report; explains why consumers would benefit from ordering their credit report; delineates other instances where consumers are eligible to receive a free report; and explains what to do if the consumer finds inaccuracies or errors in the report. As of September 1, 2005, free reports are available in all states, U.S. territories and possessions, and the District of Columbia.

Credit Union Offers Public Seminar on Credit Scoring

One regional credit union in Northeast Florida offered a free Credit Scoring Seminar to the public in August 2004 and another credit scoring seminar in the fall of 2005. Credit Scoring seminars are taught by credit union representatives and are intended to educate attendees on how to read credit reports, improve their individual credit score, identify mistakes, and settle disputes. Credit union membership eligibility is extended to everyone in Northeast Florida and all members of the public are invited to attend the credit union's free credit scoring seminars.

Large Bank Provides Classes and Materials on Credit Management

One center was created to support consumer demand for much needed financial and credit education through funds provided by a major bank. This center helps families achieve their financial goals by teaching them how to manage money and use credit wisely. A core component of the center's public awareness campaign is designed to educate consumers on the importance of knowing one's credit score. The center also conducts adult financial literacy workshops nationwide and maintains a credit and financial education Web site.

Summary

American consumers can become efficient managers of credit if they are equipped with a solid understanding of and comfort level with the credit system, its terminology, and the institutions involved in personal credit and credit reporting. Individuals also should be aware of their rights under the FCRA, understand how to check the accuracy of their credit reports, and learn how to fix potential credit report errors or other such problems through the credit dispute process.

2. Using Reputable Credit Counseling Services

Even for those who understand the credit process, knowing what to do during a time of specific financial difficulty can be particularly trying. Many consumers do not know to seek out credit counseling when it is needed most.

For American consumers experiencing financial problems, reputable and effective credit counseling services not only provide assistance in negotiating with creditors on behalf of the consumer, but also help to educate the consumer on how to manage personal finances and avoid future credit problems. Reputable credit counseling services employ counselors whom they certify and train in consumer credit, money and debt management, and budgeting. Moreover, non-profit credit counseling organizations have a legal obligation to provide education and counseling to consumers.[53]

Effective counseling services help consumers understand how to qualify for, shop for, obtain, and maintain credit. By counseling individuals on issues, such as establishing credit, debt-to-income ratios, credit history and score, comparing terms, timely repayment, credit management, and debt consolidation, credit counselors, can empower credit holders. Credit counseling efforts also can provide specific strategies for resolutions and understanding consumer protection and consumer rights. As advocates, counselors can contact lenders to discuss options in time of financial stress and help identify agencies to contact for consumer credit issues and specific complaints.

But not all credit counseling organizations provide these services. Some charge high fees, not all of which are disclosed, or urge consumers to make voluntary contributions that can cause them to fall deeper in debt. Many of these organizations claim that a debt management plan is the only option for the consumer – before those counselors spend time reviewing the consumer's financial situation – and many offer little or no consumer education and counseling. Moreover, just because a credit counseling organization says that it is non-profit does not guarantee that its services are free or affordable, or that its services are legitimate.[54]

Unfortunately, in recent years, there has been a growth in deceptive practices in the credit counseling marketplace. The FTC and some state Attorneys General recently took action against several companies that called themselves credit counseling organizations. The FTC and the state Attorneys General said that these companies deceived consumers about the cost, nature, and benefits of the services they offered; some companies even misrepresented their nonprofit status.[55]

The IRS included credit counseling agencies in its 2005 "Dirty Dozen" report in order to remind taxpayers that they should be careful with those credit counseling agencies that push debt payment agreements, charge high fees, or claim to fix credit ratings.[56] Additionally, in order to ensure that non-profit credit counseling agencies are complying with the law, the IRS has made auditing these organizations a priority.

Consumers can find assistance and guidance on personal credit issues by working with reputable credit counseling services. Additionally, other consumers utilize urban-based, non-profit financial counseling agencies offering programs that address the specialized needs of inner city residents with credit issues; and Federal judicial efforts that serve Americans who have sought relief from persistent, unresolved credit problems by filing for bankruptcy protection.

Reputable Credit Counseling Services

In communities throughout the nation, American consumers turn to credit counseling services to provide the information and guidance they need to navigate difficult credit issues. A reputable credit counseling organization will negotiate on a consumer's behalf with creditors and, more importantly, will offer advice on managing money and debts.[57] Additionally, a credit counselor will help a client develop a budget, and will provide free educational materials and workshops.

Reputable credit counseling organizations employ counselors whom they certify and train in the areas of consumer credit, debt management, and budgeting.[58] They work with consumers to analyze their entire financial situation and develop a personalized plan to solve their money problems.[59] Typically, they offer follow-up sessions that are designed to monitor the consumer's budget and keep the consumer on track.

Non-profit Organization Offers Credit Counseling in Community Centers

One nonprofit organization with a presence in several major U.S. cities includes credit counseling among the financial services it provides at its inner city community centers. Visitors to these community centers can avail themselves of financial counseling to help attain economic self-sufficiency and to help the communities in which they live gain a sustained spirit of revitalization. Through ongoing collaborations and long-term partnerships with leading government, private sector, and community interests, such urban-based, non-profit centers address the specialized needs of inner city residents with credit issues, providing self help, hands on programs that allow inner city residents to work toward financial security and achieve independence.

In these community centers, trained counselors work with credit counseling program participants over a period of two weeks to six months. The program operates in the eight cities across the country where the organization has community centers. This program and others like it work to resolve issues that previously had restricted individuals from becoming depository customers at a bank. Counselors help mitigate prohibitive issues, such as those that may restrict individuals from accessing and opening traditional, low cost lines of credit and issues that impede homeownership.

Through the hands on implementation of results-oriented specialized empowerment programs—including economic empowerment, digital empowerment, and economic education—these community centers attempt to meet the specialized needs of inner city residents who are struggling to address unresolved credit issues. The program offers one-on-one credit counseling assistance to individuals, and identifies and works to eliminate the barriers that prevent those with credit problems from fulfilling their full economic potential. The goal of this credit counseling program with an emphasis on self-help is to provide consumers with a focused, assisted course of correction.

Credit Counseling and Financial Education for Bankruptcy Filers

Consumers facing serious financial problems that may lead to bankruptcy should know that a new bankruptcy law requires them to obtain credit counseling from a credit counseling agency approved by the U.S. Trustee Program (a component of the Department of Justice) within 180 days before they file for bankruptcy.

The new law also requires a consumer bankruptcy filer to attend a personal financial instruction course, after filing bankruptcy, as a condition of receiving a discharge of debt. he U.S. Trustee Program will approve financial instruction courses for this purpose, and the Bankruptcy Clerk will maintain a publicly available list of approved courses.

These provisions, which took effect on October 17, 2005, were adopted as part of the Bankruptcy Abuse Prevention and Consumer Protection Act of 2005, signed into law on April 20, 2005.

Summary

As Americans deal with increased consumer debt, confusing financial offerings, and programs offering quick fixes to financial problems, reputable credit counseling services play a unique and important role in helping Americans to manage credit successfully. Outreach efforts should promote reputable credit counseling for consumers and help link those in need to available services.

Counseling should not be seen simply as an option of last resort. Consumers should seek out credit counseling before they encounter major problems during times of financial stress, and before a financial failing or before declaring bankruptcy. Effectively used, credit counseling can help consumers avoid future financial problems.

Calls to Action

Tactics Employed: Public Awareness, Integration, and Teachable Moments

4-1 The Treasury Department will launch a multi-media campaign in the third quarter of 2006 to seek to improve credit literacy among consumers. The campaign also will invite Americans to get information about managing consumer credit at MyMoney.gov. By accessing the Web site, Americans can learn more about credit history, credit reporting, and credit scoring.

4-2 Consumers should take advantage of the credit management tools available to them such as the free annual credit reports, available at www.annualcreditreport.com and 1-877-322-8228. Consumers should review the information in their report, understand how it is used, and know how to detect errors and possible instances of identity theft.

4-3 Consumer lenders should use their unique expertise and existing distribution channels to promote credit education among their customers and the public at large. Useful efforts might include development and distribution of credit education materials, support for reputable credit counseling or financial education efforts, referrals to credit education resources, or creation and maintenance of other financial education programs. Efforts may focus on adults or youth, but such financial education efforts should be easily distinguishable from marketing efforts from the consumer's perspective.

CALLS TO ACTION (Continued)

Tactics Employed: Public Awareness, Integration, and Teachable Moments

4-4 Consumers should seek reputable credit counseling services early, when financial problems start, to avoid potential bankruptcy. Lenders and social service organizations should refer consumers to reputable credit counseling services at the onset of financial difficulties

5. CONSUMER PROTECTION

Overview

Consumers' actions move markets and can determine the difference between the success or failure of entire businesses or industries. Government consumer protection programs confront fraud, deception and privacy breaches that can shake consumer confidence and undermine consumer choice.

When consumers are scammed, they lose more than money. They can also lose faith in the marketplace. The principle of caveat emptor ("let the buyer beware") is important for all consumers to follow. A vibrant economy cannot afford to have consumers lose confidence in the marketplace.

According to the FTC, an estimated 11 percent of American adults are scammed each year. The FTC's survey of consumer fraud in the United States, released in August 2004, showed that consumers with high levels of debt are at increased risk of becoming victims of fraud.[60]

Of the four most common frauds in the survey, three are related to credit, including credit-repair scams. These frauds often target people with high debt loads or poor credit. According to the Federal Bureau of Investigation (FBI), senior citizens also are often targets of fraud.[61] The FTC, state Attorneys General, and other Federal, state and local consumer protection agencies pursue such frauds using aggressive law enforcement.

Of the threats that consumers face in the marketplace, one of the greatest is identity theft. The FTC has found that nearly 10 million people a year are victims of identify theft, which involves either misuse of existing accounts or new accounts falsely established in the victim's name. That translates into nearly $48 billion in losses to businesses, nearly $5 billion in losses to individual victims, and nearly 300 hours per victim spent trying to resolve the resulting problems. Although people who had new accounts opened in their names made up one-third of the victims, they suffered two-thirds of the harm.[62]

Identity theft was the number one topic of consumer fraud complaints to the FTC in 2004, accounting for 39 percent of the consumer fraud complaints filed that year. In fact, the FTC receives 15,000 to 20,000 contacts each week from victims and consumers who want to learn how to protect themselves from identity theft or mitigate risks.[63]

Employers and commercial entities that have databases that contain personal identification information recently have become targets of identity thieves. This represents another potential vulnerability for identity theft and another reason consumers need to become knowledgeable about identity theft and how to deal with its consequences.

Challenges

One key to reducing fraud is the delivery of messages to consumers at times when they are open to learning and changing their behaviors, such as when they have encountered financial difficulty or have been a victim of credit fraud or identity theft. Education can empower consumers to recognize, avoid, and report fraudulent or deceptive practices and is essential to consumer protection.

Issues in Consumer Protection

1. Educating Consumers about Reducing their Risk of Identity Theft

One of a consumer's most important financial assets is his or her credit history. Identity thieves seek to deprive a growing number of Americans of the good credit reputation they have tried to build. Identity theft is an insidious crime; many consumers may not even realize they have been victimized. For most, recognition of identity theft occurs when consumers receive a bill for a credit card account that they never opened, find debts on a credit report that they never incurred, notice a billing cycle where they have not received a statement, or find specific charges that they did not sign for, authorize or know anything about.

Government entities, such as the FTC, are working to ensure that Americans are better informed about identity theft. Through public-private partnerships, consumers continue to learn more about the tell-tale signs of identity theft, preventive steps, individual legal rights, and how to exercise these rights if an incident has occurred. National public awareness campaigns also are instrumental in helping Americans to continue to receive important messages about consumer protection.

Public education initiatives such as those established by the FTC, the Treasury Department, the U.S. Postal Inspection Service, and the public-private steering committee that produces the *National Consumer Protection Week* are particularly useful in highlighting identity theft issues.

Federal Trade Commission

The FTC has taken the lead among Federal agencies in the development and dissemination of consumer information about identity theft, both in English and in Spanish. To increase consumer awareness and to help them minimize the risk of identity theft, the FTC published a booklet, *ID Theft: What It's All About?* Another FTC booklet, *Take Charge: Fighting Back Against Identity Theft*, is a comprehensive victim recovery guide that describes what steps to take, legal rights, how to handle specific problems one may encounter on the way to clearing one's name, and what to watch for in the future. This guide also includes the ID Theft Affidavit, a form developed by consumer victims, law enforcers, and credit grantors for victims to use when disputing unauthorized accounts with creditors. Many of the FTC's identity theft and credit publications include information about consumers' credit rights under the FACT Act.

The FTC also manages the Identity Theft Data Clearinghouse, the Federal government's central source of information on identity theft and its database for identity theft complaints. The FTC supports a toll-free hotline (1-877-IDTHEFT), and a secure complaint form at www.consumer. gov/idtheft.

The FTC's consumer and business education campaign on identity theft has included other materials, media mailings, radio public service announcements, and guest interviews on local and national radio and television programs. The FTC's tips for consumers on reducing their risk of identity theft or dealing with its aftermath have been repeated in thousands of radio and television broadcasts, newspaper and magazine articles, and Web sites.

Indeed, numerous law enforcement agencies, consumer protection organizations, and financial institutions have printed, distributed or repackaged the FTC's consumer information on identity theft. A national association of retirees helped enhance the FTC identity theft campaign by co-branding *ID Theft: What It's All About*. The association printed 500,000 copies of the brochure in English and 30,000 copies in Spanish, and distributed the material through its state offices at events, forums, fairs, and "consumer universities." A major supermarket chain, the SSA, the FDIC, the U.S. Secret Service, and two national credit card companies are among other entities that have customized the FTC's information and distributed its materials to audiences under those organizations' brands.

U.S. Department of the Treasury

The Treasury Department released a public report entitled *The Use of Technology to Combat Identity Theft* which focuses on available biometric technologies used to verify customers when they engage in financial transactions. This report also examines various non-biometric technologies financial institutions currently use to deter and detect the crime of identity theft. The Treasury Department anticipates continued improvements in non-biometric technologies along with the increasing use of biometric security and identity products on a case-by-case basis, but finds that biometrics are "not a silver bullet" for reducing identity theft.

In 2004, the Treasury Department, working with other parts of the Federal government and with the financial services sector, released a report entitled *Lessons Learned by Consumers, Financial Sector Firms, and Government Agencies During the Recent Rise of Phishing Attacks*. This publication, available at www.treas.gov/offices/domestic-finance/financial-institution/cip/pdf/fbiic-fsscc-report-05-2005.pdf, describes measures consumers can take to prevent falling victim to phishing and how to respond if they receive a phishing email or become a victim.

U.S. Postal Inspection Service

The U.S. Postal Inspection Service works with Federal, state, and local law enforcement partners and with other government and industry stakeholders to help prevent, investigate and prosecute identity crimes. U.S. Postal Inspectors are charged with investigating identity and financial crimes that involve the U.S. mail. The Postal Inspection Service has produced and disseminated a DVD entitled *Identity Crisis*, which presents a dramatic look at a couple victimized by identity theft, the criminals who defrauded them, and the devastating aftermath

The also provides tips on how individuals can protect themselves proactively against identity crimes and the steps they can take in the event they become victims.

U.S. Department of the Treasury DVD

The Treasury Department developed a DVD to educate consumers about how to deter and detect identity theft and what measures to take if they become victims. *Identity Theft: Outsmarting the Crooks* examines the costly crime of identity theft for which consumers spent more than 250 million hours last year repairing the damage to their credit records. In addition to what it costs consumers, commercial and financial firms lose billions annually. A real life victim's story highlights how important it is that victims of identity theft act quickly to resolve their situations. Panel discussions emphasize the value of industry, government, and consumer collaboration to combat this crime online and in the physical world.

In the DVD, financial sector representatives and government officials discuss what identity theft is, how identity thieves go about stealing identities, and specific steps we as individuals can take to safeguard our sensitive information. Viewers will learn that common sense actions like destroying documents with sensitive information before throwing them out or checking their credit reports at least once a year can help stop the thieves. Viewers will also find that filing a police report can help to expedite a victim's recovery from identity theft. A resource library contains additional information, brochures, forms, and Web sites to help consumers.

In the first quarter of 2006, the Treasury Department will make the DVD available to the public through the MyMoney.gov Web site and the 1-888-MyMoney toll-free hotline.

National Consumer Protection Week

National Consumer Protection Week (NCPW) is designed to highlight consumer protection and education efforts around the country. Every February a steering committee of government agencies and public and private sector groups partner to select and profile a timely topic of consumer interest. For example, for the 2005 campaign, organizations partnered to help educate consumers and businesses about identity theft. A theme of the 2004 NCPW dealt with the benefits of financial literacy. Each year, the NCPW steering committee Web site offers a "turnkey" press kit, with resources including sample news releases, letters to the editor, op-eds, radio public service announcements, posters, educational materials, and promotional ideas.

NCPW is organized by a coalition of organizations, including the FTC, the Federal Citizen Information Center, the Federal Communications Commission, the FDIC, the U.S. Department of Justice's Office for Victims of Crime, the U.S. Postal Service, the U.S. Postal Inspection Service, a national association targeted to consumer agency leaders, a national organization for consumers, a national association for retirees, a national organization representing local businesses, a major consumer rights and protection agency, a national consumer federation, the National Association of Attorneys General, a national association targeted to consumer affairs leaders, the California Office of Privacy Protection, the Ohio Attorney General's Office, a non-profit resource center with a focus on identity theft, and a non-profit clearinghouse that addresses privacy rights issues.

Summary

Education is a consumer's first line of defense against a variety of unfair, deceptive and misleading practices in the marketplace. Consumers can learn how to avoid, identify, and report a variety of threats by accessing educational materials through the media, state and local government agencies, advocacy and community-based organizations, schools, and other trusted sources.

2. Guarding against Fraudulent Business Opportunities

Some Americans can be taken in by fictitious business opportunities and other money-making schemes, where fraudsters try to gain consumers' financial information and access to their financial resources. These schemes pose real dangers to Americans seeking to invest in a business opportunity.

The FTC uses aggressive law enforcement to put fraudsters out of business and creative education tools to raise public awareness of fraudulent business opportunities. Fraudulent business opportunities can have potentially long term effects on consumers. The FTC is expanding its efforts to alert consumers to recognize, avoid and report frauds of all kinds, including advance fee loan scams, credit card loss protection plans, and credit repair scams.

The FTC's *Project Biz Opp Flop* illustrates the agency's approach to raising awareness of one major consumer protection issue.

Project Biz Opp Flop

Business opportunity scams appeal to the optimist in everyone, with their exhortations to "Be your own boss!" They are of particular concern to the FTC because they often prey upon consumers who are trying to build a solid economic future and therefore, those least able to afford being ripped-off. The FTC attacks these scams on two fronts: through coordinated law enforcement actions and consumer education.

For example, the FTC recently launched *Operation Biz Opp Flop*, a collaborative civil and criminal law enforcement effort to crack down on business opportunity fraud, including franchise and work-at-home scams. The effort included six FTC cases aimed at schemes that defrauded consumers out of approximately $100 million dollars, and more than 100 additional civil and criminal actions brought by the U.S. Department of Justice, the U.S. Postal Inspection Service, and 14 states.

To reach consumers who use the Internet to find business opportunities, the effort also included launching a "teaser" Web site that provides valuable information on how to avoid falling victim to a business opportunity scheme. The site for *Sundae Station* (www.wemarket4u.net/sundaestation) looks like a pitch for a "can't miss" business opportunity for an ice cream sundae vending machine. The site contains typical claims of fast money with minimal effort. Once consumers click on any of the links, they learn the ad is actually a consumer education piece posted by the FTC with guidance about recognizing and avoiding business opportunity rip-offs. The *Sundae Station* teaser site is part of a larger consumer education campaign that includes media outreach along with brochures, electronic cards, public service messages for the classified ad columns of newspapers, and short newspaper feature.

The cooperation between the FTC and law enforcement authorities—and the resulting press coverage—sends a clear message to business opportunity scammers: law enforcement authorities are watching, and if you choose to engage in fraud, they will find you and shut you down. As a result of aggressive public campaigns, such scam artists also are beginning to recognize that jail time may await them for their misdeeds.

Summary

Public education efforts should accompany every consumer protection law enforcement announcement. Such outreach activities play an important role in educating consumers about frauds in the marketplace, as well as how to recognize and avoid fraud, and what to do if they have been victimized.

3. Safeguarding Senior Citizens from Targeted Consumer Threats

Many criminals choose to prey on older Americans. Through education efforts and engagement campaigns launched by organizations such as the Attorney General's Offices of Florida and Kentucky, more seniors are better able to defend themselves against consumer fraud, including identity theft.

Attorney General's Office of Florida

Recognizing the specific fraud threats to senior citizens and seeking to educate residents on how to avoid such risks, the Attorney General's Office of Florida established the *Seniors vs. Crime Project*. Run by volunteers, this seniors-focused program reinforces the message of crime prevention and provides specific means for Florida's senior population to be alerted to consumer fraud and other such criminal acts. To date, *Seniors vs. Crime* has trained more than 2,000 volunteers throughout the state to assist in this public education effort.

Seniors vs. Crime was started to offer crime prevention seminars to Florida's older residents while providing comprehensive training for law enforcement officers and other criminal justice practitioners in understanding how their work is impacted by Florida's aging population. Since its launch, the program has established storefronts where seniors can visit to report potential frauds or seek additional information.

Attorney General's Office of Kentucky

The Attorney General's Office of Kentucky works in collaboration with local law enforcement officials to operate a consumer protection prevention program entitled *Senior Crime College*. The *Senior Crime College* is designed to teach seniors how to recognize potential crimes before they happen by making them aware of the techniques perpetrators commonly use, and who to alert if they identify a scam or are victimized. The program, started in 1998, has educated thousands of Kentucky's senior citizens on various consumer protection topics such as telemarketing fraud, home improvement and repair fraud, identity theft, and sweepstakes fraud. On average, there are about four programs a month where representatives from the Attorney General's office and local law enforcement officials travel to senior centers and community facilities. To complement the *Senior Crime College*, the Attorney General's office also disseminates a crime prevention handbook for seniors.

Summary

Recognizing that senior citizens are frequently targeted by perpetrators of fraud, general consumer protection efforts by private and public sector organizations need to pay attention to the specific needs of seniors. Programs, materials, and outreach efforts should address seniors explicitly and make reporting accessible to those who have been victimized.

CALLS TO ACTION

Tactics Employed: Public Awareness, Partnerships, and Quality Materials

5-1 Americans should learn more about preventing and recovering from identity theft through the use of Federal government materials. The media, private companies and non-profits can help with the Federal government's efforts to raise awareness by directing consumers to MyMoney.gov and www.consumer.gov.

5-2 In the first quarter of 2006, the Treasury Department will make the DVD, entitled *Identity Theft: Outsmarting the Crooks*, available to the public through the MyMoney.gov Web site and the 1-888-MyMoney toll-free hotline.

6. TAXPAYER RIGHTS

Overview

For virtually all Americans, understanding our rights and responsibilities as taxpayers is an essential component of financial literacy. As the American economy has evolved, tax code provisions have proliferated in number and complexity. Navigating the complicated maze of code has become increasingly challenging for many. The task of simplifying the code is an important issue, attracting attention from the highest levels of government. President George W. Bush made it part of his reform agenda, outlining his plan within the 2005 State of the Union Address: "Year after year, Americans are burdened by an archaic, incoherent Federal tax code. I've appointed a bipartisan panel to examine the tax code from top to bottom. And when their recommendations are delivered, you [United States Congress] and I will work together to give this nation a tax code that is pro-growth, easy to understand, and fair to all."

In January 2005, the President appointed a bipartisan Advisory Panel on Federal Tax Reform, under the leadership of Senators Connie Mack and John Breaux, to make recommendations to make the tax code fairer for all Americans, simpler so everyone can understand it, and more pro-growth, to help boost our economy. The panel was also asked to draft recommendations that were revenue neutral and that considered the importance of homeownership and charitable giving. The Panel held meetings all over the country; the members listened to experts, economists, lawyers, and average taxpayers; they studied all the information that was presented to them, and they have made bold recommendations. The recommendations were presented to U.S. Treasury Secretary John W. Snow on November 1, 2005, which began the dialogue that will help shape the future of tax policy. Their advice is the starting point, and the Treasury Department is reviewing their recommendations and considering them carefully before making recommendations to the President.

Given the complexity of Federal tax laws, many Americans currently rely on third-party assistance (paid and voluntary) to file their tax returns. In fact, more than 60 percent of all Americans use tax preparation services and spend more than $140 billion annually on these services. Many taxpayers focus strictly on meeting their obligations — that is, paying the amount owed to the government. However, taxpayers have rights as well as obligations, and financially educated taxpayers are aware of both. The Federal tax code states that some people, such as persons with disabilities, senior citizens, those with low- to middle-income, the unemployed, and other groups, may be eligible for various benefits available through Federal programs and through tax incentives. Such support is often critical, in some cases bringing low-income taxpayers one step closer to financial stability.

Challenges

Many taxpayers do not receive the tax benefit for which they are eligible. To understand why this is the case, two primary factors must be considered. First, taxpayers — both individuals and businesses — do not automatically receive benefits; they must take direct action to initiate or claim the benefit. This, however, raises the second point — taxpayers must first be aware of those benefits for which they are eligible. Public awareness campaigns and educational initiatives must squarely address the issue of making taxpayers cognizant of the benefits for which they qualify under the Federal tax code.

Taxpayer rights are compromised when taxpayers are unaware of the full range and scope of available programs and initiatives. Increased public awareness offers the potential to maximize taxpayers' access to resources that simplify the tax payment process and increase utilization of programs and rights for which taxpayers may be eligible.

Issues in Taxpayer Rights

1. Helping Individuals to Identify and Utilize Available Programs and Services

Individuals qualify for tax benefits for a host of reasons. Persons with disabilities and/or their caretakers, senior citizens, low- to middle-income or unemployed individuals, and others all may be eligible to receive valuable benefits. Tax benefits are organized on both national and community-based levels and may take the form of tax credits, tax preparation assistance or even direct advocacy.

Tax Credits

When taxpayers fail to exercise their rights, billions of dollars in unclaimed benefits are forfeited. Those who do exercise their rights realize a significant return: that is, 21 million low-income, working American taxpayers do receive approximately $38 billion by claiming the Earned Income Tax Credit (EITC), a measure designed to aid low-income Americans.[64] Yet millions of taxpayers eligible for the credit do not claim it, effectively forfeiting billions of dollars each year. The EITC is just one of many such credits available to benefit low-income, working Americans.

Other taxpayers are aware that they qualify for some benefits but disregard their eligibility for other benefits. For example, taxpayers who receive Supplemental Security Income (SSI) often neglect other benefits that they are entitled to through the Federal tax code. Further, a 2004 poll found that 83 percent of persons with disabilities never claimed available tax credits and/or deductions related to work, and less than half of persons with disabilities who own homes claimed available home mortgage interest deductions.[65]

National Volunteer Tax Preparation Programs

Those who are entitled to EITC, SSI, and other Federal benefits can maximize their opportunities by turning to volunteer tax preparers, often available through a range of Federal, non profit and faith-based organizations. For instance, low-income workers can seek assistance from the IRS's *Voluntary Income Tax Assistance* (VITA) program.

VITA provides aid to those who need help preparing their income tax returns by linking taxpayers to volunteers trained to prepare basic Federal income tax returns. VITA offers free tax help to people whose incomes are $36,000 or less. Volunteers sponsored by various organizations receive training to prepare basic tax returns in communities across the country. VITA sites are generally located at community and neighborhood centers, libraries, schools, shopping malls and other convenient locations. In some locations, participants also are able to receive free electronic filing of completed tax returns. The VITA Web site is www.irs.gov/newsroom/article/0,,id= 108 104,00.html.

The IRS also sponsors programs to provide taxpayer assistance for key target populations, including, for example, senior citizens and military personnel. The Tax Counseling for the Elderly (TCE) program provides free tax assistance to people 60 or older, while Tax-Aide volunteer-counselors offer tax advice to low-to-middle income taxpayers, particularly those 60 or older during the filing season. The Armed Forces Tax Council offers tax program coordinators for members of the Army, Air Force, Navy, Marine Corps and Coast Guard. Through military VITA sites, service personnel can receive free tax advice, tax preparation, and assistance to military members and their families worldwide. Moreover, people with disabilities can receive tax benefit information and assistance through a collaborative national tax campaign and local social services agencies.

Local Social Services Organization Offers Free Tax Filing to Low-Income Taxpayers in Florida

Often, free tax preparation assistance exists at the local level. Such services deliver assistance to those who need support to successfully navigate current tax code provisions.

For example, taxpayers in one city in Florida who seek assistance in securing the tax benefits to which they are entitled have access to a program that enables them to turn to local organizations for help. The effort seeks to empower individuals and communities by promoting civic engagement, economic fairness and improved access to health and human services. A key purpose of the campaign is to heighten awareness of and increase the number of low-income workers in the area who claim the refundable Federal EITC.

First launched in 2002, in its first year, the program generated an additional $62 million in revenue for area residents by significantly boosting EITC filings. With the "multiplier" effect of local spending, the program's inaugural year is estimated to have had an impact of a quarter of a billion dollars on the local economy.[66] In one Florida city, the program assisted 9,258 residents in the 2004 tax season, achieving over $800,000 in saved tax preparation fees.[67] Further, the campaign helps consumers file tax returns electronically and encourages unbanked taxpayers to open bank or credit union accounts to allow direct deposit of tax refunds.

To achieve this, the program works with 6,000 community volunteers trained by the IRS who are drawn from a broad spectrum of community groups, faith-based organizations, policy makers, businesses, and individuals. Free tax preparation services are offered to consumers in need, a service that helps to increase the overall volume of community EITC filings. An additional goal of the initiative is to promote general financial education and to enhance workers' abilities to build assets by making them aware of reputable financial institutions and asset development programs.

Taxpayer Advocate Service

Individual and business taxpayers have access to useful resources — even confidential, free counsel — to resolve tax-related problems. The *Taxpayer Advocate Service* (TAS) is available to provide assistance in this area.

Although the TAS is a part of the IRS, it avoids conflict of interest through its statutory independence, and its case advocates work on behalf of taxpayers to ensure that problems are resolved properly. TAS has the authority to direct the IRS to hold off on taking certain imminent collection actions until the taxpayer has an opportunity to speak with IRS personnel about alternatives. To request the services of a TAS case advocate, taxpayers must contact TAS at their toll-free number.

In addition, all taxpayers have the right to secure representation to resolve Federal tax disputes. Depending on income level, Low-Income Taxpayer Clinics (LITCs) represent low-income taxpayers before the IRS in Federal tax disputes at no cost or for a nominal charge.

TAS also administers a grant program for LITCs. Though the clinics receive partial funding from the IRS, both the clinics and clinic volunteers are completely independent of and are not affiliated with the Federal government, and instead are operated by nonprofit organizations or academic institutions. LITCs also provide tax education and/or outreach for taxpayers who speak English as a second language. A list of LITC locations can be found on the IRS Web site.

Summary

A number of taxpayer benefits are available to Americans. By taking advantage of the credits and services described, taxpayers can better understand their rights and can optimize their personal and business tax filings. Increased education allows taxpayers to avail themselves fully of the benefits to which they are entitled under the Federal tax code.

2. Education and Outreach to Individuals and Employers

Education and outreach are essential to help make taxpayers aware of the benefits available to them as part of the Federal tax code. While some of the programs were addressed previously, this section of the *National Strategy* centers on the education and outreach aspects of these programs. Education and outreach is often appropriately tailored to respond to the needs of key constituencies, such as individuals with disabilities and those who employ or support them. Other programs identified, for example, support the specialized needs of taxpayers who reside in rural areas; while still others profile the targeted efforts of local social service agencies. Also featured are Federal efforts to increase awareness of and access to tax incentives for business.

National Campaign for Individuals with Disabilities and their Caretakers and Employers

Thirty-eight percent of working-age adults with disabilities live in households with annual incomes of under $15,000, and 30 percent of disabled working adults hold neither checking nor saving accounts.[68] Such statistics demonstrate the need to better educate those with disabilities about their eligibility for particular benefits to improve their financial standing. Community organizations play a critical role in responding to the need for increased awareness. For example, a coalition of non-profit organizations, Federal government agencies, lenders, and educational institutions recently launched a three-year, multi-faceted national campaign to inform individuals with disabilities, their families, and their employers about favorable tax provisions, financial education and other asset-building strategies.

The partnership campaign empowers disabled individuals and advances self-directed economic security by developing new publications and products on access, accommodation, benefits training, tax provisions, and technical assistance. One principal partner, a non-profit organization, also established a Web site to serve as a central location for financial information and identify credible resources for individuals with disabilities. In addition, the IRS has links to publications for individuals with disabilities at www.irs.gov.

Cooperative Extension Conducts Rural Outreach Project for Georgia Tax Filers

The *Taxpayer Education and Outreach in Rural America Project, delivered in 12 states by the Cooperative Extension*, a nationwide, non-formal educational system, provides an annual opportunity for asset building among working poor families by assisting with the correct determination of tax liabilities and credits. The program promotes taxpayer education, offers information about refundable tax credits, and makes free tax assistance available to those who reside in rural areas of the states. In addition, the program links filers to Cooperative Extension System financial literacy programs offered in partnership with the USDA-CSREES.

For the 2003 tax season, Georgia Cooperative Extension partnered with the IRS, which provided laptop computers, software, training, certification, and technical support. Staff provided one day of free tax filing assistance each week throughout the filing season at five locations plus numerous "one- day" sites arranged in partnership with local employers and other partners. As a result, in total, more than 400 tax returns were filed. In 2004, program assistants provided one day of free tax preparation per week in each of 18 counties throughout the filing season, along with numerous one-day remote sites at convenient locations to prepare 1,000 Federal and state tax returns. These filers received a total refund of $1.4 million, which they in turn spent or saved in one of 18 mostly poor, rural counties. More than half (57 percent) paid between $19 and $425 for tax preparation in 2003, with an average of $104 spent; this resulted in a combined saving of $49,572 in 2004 for some 575 filers. Use of direct deposit by filers doubled, from only 24 percent saying they used direct deposit last year to nearly half (49 percent) using it this year.

Social Services Agency in Kansas Helps Disabled Claim Tax Benefits

Social services agencies are poised to exert significant influence in their communities. For instance, one social services agency is collaborating with organizations and offices throughout Kansas to increase knowledge about and access to available financial services products among people with disabilities. The agency designed specific efforts targeted toward making individuals on SSI and Social Security Disability Insurance (SSDI) aware of the tax benefits under the Earned Income Tax Credit that they were potentially eligible for, but had not necessarily sought.

In 2003, the agency prepared returns for 97 individuals who had no filing requirement or withholdings, with 54 percent receiving tax refunds for the first time. The refunds represented $36,161 in new money for local residents. Some refunds were invested in personal savings while other funds were reinvested in the local economy.

Department of Labor Helps Businesses Employ Disabled Workers

Businesses, too, should understand benefits granted to them by the Federal tax code, for instance, those given for hiring and accommodating people with disabilities. DOL's Office of Disability Employment Policy (ODEP) has developed a *Tax Incentives for Business Fact Sheet.* This document outlines the following three tax incentives which help employers offset costs incurred in accommodating employees with disabilities: the Small Business Tax Credit, the Architectural/Transportation Tax Deduction, and the Work Opportunity Tax Credit (WOTC).[69]

Under the Small Business Tax Credit, businesses may take an annual deduction for expenses incurred to remove physical, structural and transportation barriers in the workplace to accommodate persons with disabilities.[70] WOTC provides a tax credit of up to $2,400 per new employee for employers who hire workers from one of eight targeted groups, including qualified veterans, qualified SSI recipients, high risk youth, vocational rehabilitation (VR[71]) referrals, and qualified food stamp recipients.[72]

Summary

Campaigns, programs and other outreach initiatives supported by partnerships among the Federal government, community based-organizations, non-profit organizations, and academic institutions can increase public awareness of helpful tax provisions. All Americans — individual taxpayers, and especially persons with disabilities and their caregivers and employers — benefit from increased awareness of taxpayer rights, responsibilities and assistance. Outreach efforts help individual and business taxpayers realize their financial potential under the tax law, even providing assistance in tax dispute resolution.

3. Reducing Taxpayer Risks and Costs by Encouraging Direct Deposit

Taxpayers who receive Federal benefits, such as Social Security, may be at particular risk for fraud. Because many low- and moderate-income Americans receive Federal benefits through the mail, thieves are focused on intercepting checks and sensitive information from recipients and improperly using that information.

Taxpayers can protect their Federal benefits from thieves and external threats by taking advantage of innovative programs such as direct deposit of checks. Application of successful initiatives such as the *Go Direct* campaign (detailed below) can help to equip consumers with the tools they need to take advantage of direct deposit opportunities.

Go Direct ***Campaign Increases the Safety and Convenience of Receiving Federal Benefits***

Sponsored by the Treasury Department and a Federal Reserve Bank, *Go Direct* is an initiative aimed at educating Americans on the many benefits of having their payments deposited electronically. The campaign seeks to motivate people to receive their Federal benefits in the safest, fastest and easiest way possible — direct deposit. *Go Direct's* public education campaign is designed to motivate more Americans to deposit their Federal benefit payments, such as Social Security and SSI, directly into their accounts with financial institutions.

The goal of the program is to help people get their Federal benefits in a way that is simple, safe and secure. Direct deposit is less burdensome for recipients because payments are deposited straight into the recipient's personal account, eliminating the need to hand-carry checks to a bank, credit union, or other depository institution. Since payment is sent and received electronically, the process is faster than traditional payment methods, giving participants greater financial flexibility. The opportunity for criminals to steal checks in the mail is completely removed, eliminating the risk of mail fraud and reducing the risk of identity theft.

Direct deposit generates significant cost saving to the financial system in general, approximately 75 cents per payment of paper checks, multiplied by millions of benefit payments per month. With the Treasury Department issuing nearly 160 million benefit checks each year, direct deposit has the potential to save taxpayers about $120 million annually.

Despite direct deposit's attractive benefits, currently millions of Americans — many senior citizens and disabled populations — still do not take advantage of the opportunity, choosing instead to receive their Social Security and other Federal benefits in the mail. Efforts to increase direct deposit will benefit today's seniors and future generations in numerous ways, and, as such, the Treasury Department remains committed to encouraging more people to take advantage of the many benefits of direct deposit through the *Go Direct* campaign.

Summary

American taxpayers can take full advantage of the Federal benefits available to them, without fear of fraud or theft, by utilizing important financial tools such as direct deposit. In addition to the security benefits of direct deposit, the system also is highly cost effective.

4. Taking Advantage of Important, New Benefits to Realize Financial Saving

As the population continues to age, prescription drug coverage is of paramount importance to current and future retirees. Under a new Federal program, beginning January 1, 2006, prescription drug coverage is available to eligible Medicare beneficiaries. HHS' Prescription Drug Coverage public awareness campaign is an extensive outreach program that will educate consumers about the benefits they can receive from the new Medicare prescription drug plan (Medicare Part D).

Medicare Prescription Drug Coverage Public Awareness Campaign

HHS has embarked on an ambitious public awareness and education campaign to help eligible Americans understand and enroll in a Medicare prescription drug plan. Through this effort, HHS will distribute handbooks to all Medicare recipients, make information available on the plan through its Web site and toll-free telephone numbers, and offer free personalized counseling through the State Health Insurance Assistance Program and other community-based organizations.

Under this new benefit, Medicare recipients can receive drug coverage by enrolling in a prescription drug plan that contracts with Medicare.

To gain access to this new coverage, individuals must specifically enroll in a Medicare prescription drug plan. The initial open enrollment period for this plan runs from November 15, 2005, through May 16, 2006. Those enrolling after the initial cut-off are likely to pay higher monthly premiums, particularly if they do not currently have a drug plan that covers prescriptions.

Employer- and union-sponsored retiree plans may qualify for Medicare support if they continue to offer prescription drug coverage

Summary

To better encourage enrollment in the *Medicare Prescription Drug Coverage* plan, enhanced education efforts will be undertaken to increase public awareness and understanding of the benefits.

CALLS TO ACTION

Tactics Employed: Public Awareness, Partnerships, Quality Materials

6-1 Community groups including social service organizations, professional organizations, and faith-based organizations should take advantage of the IRS's Voluntary Income Tax Assistance program.

6-2 In 2006, the Treasury Department and a Federal Reserve Bank will continue the national public education campaign, *Go Direct*. The campaign is designed to encourage Americans who receive Federal benefit payments, particularly Social Security, to use direct deposit. On an annual basis, the program will be assessed by the agencies to determine its effectiveness and viability.

6-3 The Department of Health and Human Services will continue its public awareness campaign on the new Medicare drug benefit that encourages seniors to enroll in the program. The public awareness campaign began on November 15, 2005 and continues until May 16, 2006. The campaign provides eligible taxpayers with easy access to information regarding enrollment.

7. INVESTOR PROTECTION

Overview

Effective investor education can help all Americans become better positioned to achieve personal financial security and reach saving and investing goals such as homeownership and college education for their children. Over the long term, effective participation in our financial markets is critical to reaching these goals, as well as to achieving overall retirement security. A working knowledge of basic investing concepts will substantially improve an investor's financial future even if the investor participates in the markets only through a defined contribution retirement plan. Given that a recent survey showed that only 40 percent of investors said they "know most of what they need to make good decisions,"[73] it is clear that more investor education will benefit most Americans.

Beyond helping investors understand financial concepts, increased investor education can yield significant economic and social benefits. When consumers have the opportunity and ability to invest, they infuse the markets with vital capital that help businesses and economies grow stronger. In turn, these investments in the economy ensure that new and creative technologies have a chance to develop and flourish. Saving and investing can also help individuals and families build wealth and become more stable and secure. By actively promoting and supporting financial education at all levels — from the basics to the most complex concepts — regulators, securities professionals, and others can play a key role in assuring that all investors get the facts they need to invest wisely and avoid costly mistakes.

An important component of investor education is helping investors understand the salient characteristics of investment products. Fees and costs are significant attributes for any investment, and particularly for those held over time. While regulators do make available free resources to help Americans understand characteristics of various investments, including information on costs and fees, both public and private sectors can do more in this important area.

While investing offers significant potential rewards, it is not without risk, including the possibility of fraud. Unfortunately, financial scam artists prey on the willingness of some Americans to allow emotion to cloud their judgment. Americans lose millions of dollars each year to crooks who engage in affinity fraud and other financial crimes, lying about themselves nd the products they sell.[74] Increasingly in our global economy, these predators may be located off-shore and may not be subject to U.S. laws. Educated investors are the best defense against investment fraud, because knowledgeable consumers are equipped to ask questions and steer clear of scams.

Challenges

Americans can benefit financially by increasing their understanding of diversification, compound interest, and how to evaluate financial products. An enormous amount of high-quality education material is available for free, primarily through the Internet. Yet many of these excellent materials are underutilized and not widely disseminated.

These challenges can be overcome by educating investors so that they are better able to make appropriate financial choices, understand and evaluate financial products, and protect themselves against fraud.

Issues in Investor Protection

1. Equipping Consumers with Unbiased, Neutral Investment Information

To have the best chance for achieving personal financial goals, it is important for investors to have access to unbiased investor education materials. These materials should help investors understand the questions they should ask about investments and their investment professionals, where to seek additional information, and where to turn for help and advice.

Organizations such as the SEC, the CFTC, and state securities regulators are devoted to investor protection are particularly useful sources of this kind of neutral, unbiased investor information, some of which may also be developed through funding from court settlements. State securities regulators and trade associations for industry professionals have created several financial education campaigns that deliver sought-after information through Web sites and other programs. Finally, some organizations have partnered to develop and disseminate tailored messages on investing for African American and Hispanic communities.

Securities and Exchange Commission Provides Investor Education Resources

The SEC produces a wide variety of helpful publications, calculators, and other materials aimed at helping investors make informed investment decisions. Publications include *Get the Facts on Saving and Investing, Invest Wisely: An Introduction to Mutual Funds, and Variable Annuities: What You Should Know*. The SEC does not copyright any of its investor education materials and makes them freely available to all. The SEC's Web site (www.sec. gov) also gives investors interactive tools to help evaluate their investment decisions, linking to more than half a dozen interactive tools from other Federal agencies, self-regulatory organizations, and non-profit educational organizations.

Through the Internet, the SEC allows investors to easily check out their investment professionals, in a page entitled "Check Out Your Broker or Adviser." This page shows investors how to access free public databases containing disciplinary and other information about brokers and investment advisers. It recommends that investors call their state securities regulator for more information, and provides a link to a list of relevant phone numbers.

Most brokerage account agreements require investors to settle any disputes with their broker through arbitration rather than the courts. The SEC educates investors on how to file an arbitration claim and how to find a lawyer specializing in arbitration claims. Law schools in several states provide some investors with legal representation through arbitration or mediation clinics. These clinics may be able to help investors who have smaller claims and who are unable to hire a lawyer. The SEC helps investors contact these programs to find the assistance they need.

Commodity Futures Trading Commission Provides Online Primer

The CFTC provides consumers with a wealth of background information and tools to educate new commodity investors. The CFTC resources provide investors with ongoing and real-time tools that help detect potential fraudulent activity. Through the CFTC Web site (www.CFTC. gov), the page entitled "Before You Trade" introduces investors to the basics of futures trading and the paramount need to perform background research on the company or individual with whom they choose to invest, as well as links that provide direct access to publications about trading. The Web site also provides access to online resources for broker registration and background information. CFTC consumer advisories are issued to protect nvestors against possible fraud and lists valuable precautions investors should take before committing funds.

North American Securities Administrators Association

State securities regulating organizations serve as the voice of state and provincial security regulators and focus efforts on investor protection. These organizations are a source of consumer information on avoiding investment fraud. Investor education resources available on their Web sites include links to the securities regulator in each state. Additionally, to encourage investors to take down the specifics of any conversation they have with their investment broker, a free investor checklist identifies the fundamental questions an investor should ask before investing. This resource also provides tips to consumers, such as hanging up on any unsolicited telephone offers to buy securities.

Investor Education Funds from Court Settlements

In 2003 and 2004, settlements of Federal court litigation matters by securities regulators resulted in court approval of $85 million, to be paid over five years toward investor education. Of this total, $30 million has been specifically designated to state securities regulators for investor education purposes and $55 million for Federal efforts. The settlements involved conflicts of interest between the research and investment banking operations of the nation's top investment firms, with eight firms contributing the $85 million.

State Securities Regulators Conduct Outreach and Education Programs

Securities regulators in various states have also developed investor education campaigns. For instance, securities regulators in Florida developed a comprehensive public education initiative that uses public outreach, a media campaign, and a Web site on personal finance matters to communicate its message effectively. This effort is a result of an innovative partnership between private sector groups and the Florida Department of Financial Services.

Throughout Oklahoma, investor education is being integrated with existing financial curricula, trainings, workshops, and media opportunities, thanks to *Winning through Investment Strategies and Education* (WISE). WISE was created to customize and expand the Financial Literacy 2010 teaching guide for use in Oklahoma. (Financial Literacy 2010 is a joint project to promote financial literacy, sponsored by state securities agencies and other entities.) Established by the Oklahoma Department of Securities and a university outreach program, WISE successfully uses television and radio programs, free workshops for newly married couples, a teachers institute, an intergenerational stock camp, and free workshops for pre-retirement groups to equip Oklahomans with the investment knowledge they need to succeed.

Investment Education Programs Targeted toward African Americans and Hispanics

Four organizations joined together to create a program to strengthen investor awareness specifically in the African American and Hispanic communities. Mutual fund industry professionals deliver free education and information about personal investing at workshops and conferences across the country, at Historically Black Colleges and Universities, and in interactive Web courses in English and Spanish.

Trade Association Sponsors Web Site for Investors

Industry trade associations can help provide information to investors. For instance, one trade association foundation sponsors a Web site with information on investing and saving for retirement. The Web site provides free information on homeownership, how markets work, diversification, and principles of asset allocation.

Summary

Effective education can help investors achieve long-term financial well-being. Through effective investor education, Americans can learn to understand their own personal risk tolerance, investment objectives, and time horizon to maximize investment opportunities. Many financial services entities and community organizations focus on helping to educate investors. State and Federal regulators provide excellent resources for all consumers.

2. Encouraging Greater Understanding of Investment Characteristics, Particularly Fees

Understanding how to research and effectively compare characteristics of various investments is a critical component of investor education. Investors should fully understand the types of costs, fees, and expenses that may be charged against their accounts and the impact of those amounts over time. Even small amounts can result in to a significant total on an investment held for many years.

The SEC has a Mutual Fund Cost Calculator on its Web site, while the The National Association of Securities Dealers (NASD) has a Mutual Fund and an Exchange Traded Fund Expense Analyzer. These easy-to-navigate sites allow investors to compare fees, expenses, and other costs of owning these products, and information is available free of charge. Additionally, DOL has information on fees for those participating in retirement plans.

SEC's Mutual Fund Cost Calculator

The SEC created its Mutual Fund Cost Calculator to enable investors to easily compare fund costs and assess their impact. Available free of charge at www.sec.gov, this Internet-based tool takes the math and mystery out of questions like: "Am I better off buying a no-load fund with yearly expenses of 1.75 percent or a fund with a front-end sales charge of 3.5 percent and yearly expenses of 0.9 percent?"

The cost calculator estimates mutual fund ownership costs by including sales charges (loads), annual operating expenses paid by investors, and "foregone earnings" (money that could have been earned had those fees been invested instead).

National Association of Securities Dealers

The NASD offers investors online information through its Mutual Fund and an Exchange Traded Fund (ETF) expense analyzers. The analyzers are free tools to help compare how sales loads, fees, commissions, and other fund expenses can reduce returns on mutual funds and ETFs. The analyzers allow consumers to calculate the expenses of up to three funds or classes of a single fund at the same time. The organization makes its mutual fund expense analyzer available without charge to securities firms for use on their Intranets as a tool for brokers and on their public Web sites for use by their customers. In addition, a uniform fee disclosure form developed to help employers compare the fees of prospective providers for their plans is available on the DOL's Web site at www.dol.gov.

U.S. Department of Labor Offers Resources to Explain 401(k)s

Those participating in 401(k) retirement plans can also look to the DOL for valuable information concerning fees. The DOL has developed materials to help both employers who sponsor 401(k) plans and employees who participate in 401(k) plans understand investment fees and expenses. These materials are available at www.dol.gov/ebsa/publications. The materials help consumers understand that some fees in 401(k) plans are paid by the employer, but others are typically paid by the participant in the form of net total return for their plan account. The DOL provides various compliance assistance materials and information relating to free seminars conducted by the DOL addressing fiduciary responsibilities regarding plan investments and fees.

In addition, a uniform fee disclosure form developed to help employers compare the fees of prospective roviders for their plans is available on the DOL's Web site at www.dol.gov.

Summary

Investors should review and understand the costs, fees and expenses associated with various investment products. Investors need to understand the impact these fees and expenses may have on the potential growth of their investment vehicle. This can be achieved through public education and widespread dissemination of effective information.

3. Protecting Investors from Fraud through Increased Education Efforts

Knowledge is one of the best defenses against investment fraud. Securities regulators caution investors to investigate before they invest. Fraudsters rely on people not researching investments before they invest. In fact, if it sounds too good to be true, it probably is. Many free resources make it easy to investigate companies, products, securities professionals, and promoters before making an investment.

Effectively researching and evaluating investment choices is key to helping Americans avoid fraud. The SEC helps Americans understand what investment fraud looks like, and how to avoid it. The CFTC warns would-be investors about potential commodities and futures fraud.

SEC Uses Interactive Tool to Teach Investors about Fraud

The SEC launched a series of Internet-based initiatives to reach out to would-be investors when they are most vulnerable. By using fake scam Web sites, the SEC shows consumers how easy it can be for scam artists to gain email addresses, phone numbers, mailing addresses, and even bank account numbers, wire transfer instructions, and credit card information from potential investors. The SEC individually answers all inquiries coming in from these sites, and in many cases must invest significant time to convince consumers that these investment offers are too good to be true and fictitious.

The SEC first began this approach when it launched www.McWhortle.com, a site that purported to be "an established and well- known manufacturer" with a revolutionary product it planned to produce with the money raised through an initial public offering. In reality, the company did not exist (it was made up by the SEC), and any consumer who tried to "invest now" was greeted with an educational message warning of the danger of such scams. Within weeks of its launch, the Web site received more than 1.5 million hits and the McWhortle Webmaster (actually SEC staff) received more than 500 e-mails, nearly all of which were overwhelmingly positive about the fake opportunity. The SEC has worked with teachers to include McWhortle in teaching modules and curricula, using it as a tool for separating the good from the bad on the Internet.

The SEC also publishes brochures, in print and on its Web site, on how to avoid investment fraud. Additionally, SEC staff conducts investor protection seminars and workshops for investor groups around the country.

Commodity Futures Trading Commission Provides Fraud Avoidance Tips

The CFTC publishes information designed to help consumers avoid commodities fraud at www.cftc.gov/opa/opaconsumeradv0404.htm. Investors are warned to be wary of any firm that offers to sell commodities or commodity futures or options, particularly where the sales pitch stresses high returns and low risks. The CFTC also warns consumers about firms that claim to have made profits for all of their customers, advising that "get-rich-quick schemes, including those involving foreign currency trading, tend to be frauds." The CFTC Web site also allows investors to electronically report any suspicious activities or transactions.

Summary

Through education, Americans can become aware of different types of fraudulent investment schemes, while becoming more savvy and knowledgeable consumers of investment products in general.

CALLS TO ACTION

Tactics Employed: Quality Materials, Public Awareness

7-1 Investors should take advantage of the wealth of high quality, neutral, and unbiased information offered free of charge.

7-2 During the meeting hosted by the Treasury Department and the Department of Labor (see 3-1), the topics of discussion will include an educational emphasis on investment fees. Attendess will discuss how to present information on fees in a clear and understandable manner.

8. THE UNBANKED

Overview

Though the opportunities to participate in the United States' banking system continue to grow, the benefits of such participation are yet unrealized: More than 10 million individuals in the United States still do not maintain traditional bank transaction, credit, saving, or investment accounts.[75] In fact, according to the FRB's 2001 *Survey of Consumer Finances*, nearly 10 percent of U.S. families do not have transaction accounts and more than 12 percent lack checking accounts.[76] Many more Americans may have transaction accounts but do not take advantage of available options that are offered to them, and instead use alternative financial service providers.

The term "unbanked" is widely used to describe individuals who do not have a transaction account with any type of traditional financial institution, not just a bank. The term also includes people who do not have accounts at credit unions, thrifts, or other traditional depository institutions. This National Strategy adopts the common, broader usage of the term "unbanked" which refers to individuals without an established relationship with a depository institution. These individuals can also be described as operating outside of the financial mainstream.[77]

According to a 2003 survey of 46 banks, more than 98 percent of the banks surveyed provided some type of financial education program; however, many of these programs pertain to people who already use financial services. For example, 96 percent of banks provided homeownership and mortgage counseling; 93 percent offered affordable mortgage programs; and 91 percent offered credit counseling. In contrast, only 57 percent of banks surveyed offered education programs that specifically target the unbanked.[78]

Challenges

Individuals who have not established a relationship with a depository institution turn away from traditional financial services for a number of reasons, including cultural differences (see Chapter 9 for more information), language barriers, a lack of trust in financial institutions, insufficient knowledge of products and services available, or insufficient assessment of their own financial needs. These individuals also tend not to use traditional depository institutions (e.g., banks, credit unions, thrifts, etc.). Many factors contribute to people's reluctance: whether a result of lack of money, an absence of convenient locations, or the (mistaken) view that writing just a few checks a month does not warrant the need for a bank account, various barriers to participation in the traditional financial system must be considered when constructing meaningful financial education efforts. One such barrier is the ready availability of alternative services, such as check cashing services.

Moreover, some depository institutions may not offer products that are suitable for many of the unbanked. For example, checking account products may require high minimum balances, which preclude low-income consumers from effectively using them. While these challenges can be overcome through industry-driven financial products and services, it is essential to establish and expand public-private and private-private partnerships committed to financial education activities specifically tailored to the unbanked. These activities might include ongoing national and local public awareness campaigns that prioritize educating those outside the financial mainstream on the availability and benefits of financial services.

Issues for the Unbanked

1. Using Banking Industry-Driven Products and Services to Increase Understanding and Utilization

Cultural differences may initially impede those outside the financial mainstream from turning to traditional financial services. In addition to some distrust of banks among the unbanked, many banking products are not well-designed to meet the needs of low-income immigrants — the largest group likely to be among those individuals considered to be unbanked. They turn instead to alternative financial services, such as wire transfer companies and currency exchanges, to send money to relatives because they may not view U.S. banks as providers of similar services. In 2004 alone, immigrants in the U.S. sent approximately $35 billion to countries in Latin America and the Caribbean — representing the biggest share of immigrants in the U.S[79] Further, monthly fees and minimum balances may inhibit or otherwise preclude low-income individuals, particularly immigrants, from opening checking accounts, in addition to mortgage products with down payment requirements.

As the products and services made available through the U.S. banking (traditional depository) system increase, opportunities exist to help individuals outside of the financial mainstream learn about and understand what is available to them through local institutions. For example, remittance programs to send money to native countries, branch offices with special services, "starter" checking accounts, fixed value contribution accounts, deposit-secured loans, secured credit cards for those with no credit history, and employer payroll debit/ATM cards may, depending on how these plans are structured, serve as good introductory services for this group.[80] A combination of traditional and nontraditional depository institution services (e.g., money orders, domestic and international wire transfers and sale of pre-paid phone cards) may also be included by the financial system as it develops and distributes the products that may help meet the needs of the unbanked.

Community-based efforts such as *Access Across America*, *First Home Club Savings Program*, and locally based saving accounts that offer matching funds enable individuals without an established relationship with a depository institution to turn to U.S. financial institutions for specific products and programs of value.

Credit Unions Reaching Out to the Unbanked through *Access Across America*

Access Across America, an initiative of the NCUA, was established to create economic empowerment and facilitate the extension of affordable financial services to individuals and communities across the nation. NCUA partners with Federal agencies to develop opportunities to assist credit unions with the resources needed to serve underserved areas. Since 2000, through the NCUA's streamlined regulatory framework, more than 700 credit unions have adopted over 1,200 underserved areas, providing access to credit union service to more than 100 million Americans. *Access Across America* has forged partnership opportunities for credit unions to make the ownership society a reality for millions of Americans who might otherwise be left out. The initiative focuses on key areas such as homeownership, *Health Savings Accounts*, small business lending, financial education and serving the underserved.

First Home Club Savings Program

For those unaccustomed to saving through traditional depository institutions, the concept represents an easy-to-implement, understandable account program designed to move individuals toward acquiring basic financial services. To introduce people to available services, banks that participate in a *First Home Club Savings Account Program* provide low- and moderate- income individuals the tools and support to help them achieve homeownership *Club* members maintain a dedicated saving account designated for the down payment and closing costs on a first home. *Club* members must participate in both group and individual education sessions. Finally, when participants complete the program, the *Club* matches their savings at a three-to-one ratio up to $5,000.

Saving Accounts with Matching Funds

Saving for a down payment on a home can be overwhelming for anyone, but particularly for those individuals who are unfamiliar with traditional depository institution saving plans. To encourage and support such saving among residents of a city in New York, the local banks along with the city housing authority encourage citizens to save by offering saving with matching funds; in this way, individuals can begin saving funds toward a down payment on a house. Participants set a saving goal and make regular deposits over a pre-determined period of time. When the individual goal is met, the housing authority, an affordable housing organization, matches the deposited funds. As an added incentive, the saving account is free of traditional service charges.

Summary

The financial industry can open new doors for individuals and strengthen local communities by developing innovative financial products and services that meet the needs of individuals without a relationship with a depository institution at the pre-banking, entry and advanced banking service levels.

2. Encouraging Collaboration and Use of Existing Relationships to Increase Familiarity with Financial System

Some immigrants harbor a distrust of the U.S. financial system, perhaps as a result of instability of the financial systems in their home countries or for other reasons. This reluctance to access financial services is exacerbated by language barriers that prevent depository institutions and other organizations from properly educating consumers on available programs and services. Other unbanked individuals may be wary of financial institutions due to distant location, past negative experiences, concern that saving will affect their ability to receive government benefits, or other factors. By working with individuals in a collegial environment, local partnerships can help people acquire the financial skills necessary to reach objectives such as securing a job, buying a house or saving toward a personal goal. This is evident in the success of efforts such as *Money Smart* and the HHS' *Assets for Independence.*

Money Smart Financial Education Program

To expand the reach of financial services to the growing ranks of those groups considered to be unbanked, the FDIC is collaborating with public- and private-sector organizations to promote *Money Smart* and the range of financial education resources and services it provides. *Money Smart* is a comprehensive adult financial education curriculum designed to help low- and moderate-income individuals outside of the financial mainstream develop financial skills and positive banking relationships. Linked with other asset building programs, the FDIC is able to provide an easily understood, multilanguage, multimedia program. *Money Smart* is available free of charge and without copyright restrictions in English, Spanish, Chinese, Korean and Vietnamese (www.fdic.gov/consumers/ consumer/moneysmart). FDIC has linked many banks to community groups through *Money Smart*, establishing nearly 1,200 public-private partnerships nationwide that have increased the reach of its financial education efforts.

At the Federal level, FDIC has partnered with the IRS to link *Voluntary Income Tax Assistance* (VITA) sites to *Money Smart* Model Sites, where financial education is taught on a regular basis and generates active participants. These partnerships work together to increase awareness among low-income consumers about eligibility for tax credits such as the Earned Income Tax Credit (EITC). VITA sites also offer free tax help to eligible wage earners and help consumers obtain applicable tax credits. In 2004, FDIC *Money Smart* Model Site partners helped 3,435 families file EITC claims totaling more than $5.1 million (an average of $1,485 per family).[81]

Also on the Federal level, FDIC has partnered with DOL's Employment and Training Administration through their one-stop career centers to offer *Money Smart* as part of their programs that target populations likely to be outside the financial mainstream, such as welfare-to-work participants, individuals with no access to mainstream financial service providers, public housing residents, immigrants and low-income homebuyers.

At the community level, *Money Smart* has brought together FDIC and a national nonprofit housing organization to help revitalize communities across the United States through financial education efforts. This organization has been using the *Money Smart* curriculum to train educators from local nonprofit organizations who will teach between 1,000 and 2,000 students each year.[82]

At the regional level, FDIC's Kansas City Region has worked with 270 partners and community development collaborators in the region to facilitate 18,000 low-income individuals' attendance at *Money Smart* classes. As a result, 9,500 low-income households, including immigrants, have opened deposit accounts and saved $2.25 million over a two-year period. These figures include 724 Individual Development Accounts (IDAs) that make two-to-one matching funds to families' deposit accounts. The funds may only be used by participants for certain purposes, such as buying a home for the first time, going to college or vocational/technical school or opening a small business. All IDA participants in some locations attend *Money Smart* classes as a requirement to access funds.[83]

Overall, *Money Smart* has helped more than over 300,000 consumers, resulting in the formation of 80,000 new depository account relationships.

Americans Enter the Financial Mainstream through U.S. Department of Health and Human Services Program

The Office of Community Services, Administration for Children and Families, HHS, administers the *Assets for Independence Program*, which currently provides grants to support more than 300 IDA[84] projects throughout the nation. Each project features strong partnership arrangements between a community- based entity or a state or local government agency and a private-sector bank or credit union. Several national banking organizations are supporting the IDA concept through their local affiliates.

IDAs are special restricted bank or credit union accounts that enable low- income individuals and families to save earned income and receive matching funds of up to $2,000 per individual. Participants use their accumulated saving plus the IDA matching funds to acquire a long-term asset, such as a first home or micro-business or to enroll for or obtain higher education. IDA customers receive financial education, and credit and debt counseling, along with other supportive services to ensure their long-term success. For many participants, the IDA is their first saving or checking account.

Summary

Financial literacy information and resources can be delivered directly to those without a relationship to a financial institution, the unbanked, through collaborative community partnerships. Both public-private and private-private partnerships can play valuable roles in this effort.

CALL TO ACTION

Tactics Employed: Quality Materials, Partnerships

8-1 Between the second quarter of 2006 and the third quarter of 2007, the U.S. Department of the Treasury, along with the Federal Deposit Insurance Corporation, the National Credit Union Administration, and the Office of the Comptroller of the Currency, will host a series of four regional conferences to share best practices on banking of the unbanked. The conferences will bring together community-based organizations, financial service providers, and Federal, state, and local regulators to broker partnerships and discuss the latest developments and strategies in bringing people into the financial mainstream.

9. MULTILINGUAL AND MULTICULTURAL POPULATIONS

Overview

Throughout the nation, minority markets serve as an important area of growth for the American economy. The financial services community looks to minority markets as areas for demonstrable growth, particularly with their projected buying power. Projections from 2004 to 2009 indicate: an Asian buying power gain of 45 percent; a Hispanic buying power gain of 45 percent; an American Indian buying power gain of 38 percent; an African American buying power gain of 33 percent; and a multi-racial buying power gain of 30 percent. By comparison, the buying power of Caucasian Americans is projected to rise by only 27 percent in the same five-year time period.[85]

Such projected increases in buying power of minority populations are expected to result in a combined minority buying power of $3 trillion by 2009.[86] However, despite minority populations' significant contribution to the national economy, the immigrants among them are less likely to participate in mainstream financial services than are native-born populations.[87] Among Mexican immigrants, 53 percent do not hold transaction accounts, while 37 percent of other Latin Americans are without accounts. Similarly, 20 percent of Asians and 17 percent of European immigrants do not hold transaction accounts.

While the homeownership rate among minority households is higher than it has ever been, minority populations still are not purchasing homes at rates similar to other groups. In the past 10 years (1995 through the first quarter of 2005), the Caucasian homeownership rate has increased from 71 percent to 76 percent, the African-American homeownership rate has increased from 43 percent to 49 percent, and the Hispanic homeownership rate has increased from 42 percent to 50 percent.[88] Similarly, from 1994 through 2004, the Indian/Aleut/Eskimo homeownership rate increased from 52 percent to 56 percent and the Asian or Pacific Islander homeownership rate rose from 51 percent to 60 percent.[89] While part of the disparity in homeownership rates across minority and Caucasian populations can be explained in part by limited access to financial services and products for those sectors of the population who reside in remote communities, fundamental cultural differences may bear a far greater impact and must be recognized. To connect effectively, financial education programs to multilingual and multicultural populations must also be accommodated.

Challenges

As minority markets become a larger and more powerful segment of the U.S. economy, it is important that minority populations take full advantage of the financial services and opportunities available to them. Whether it is because they are not participating in financial markets, doubt the possibility of homeownership, or face other hurdles, minority populations face specific challenges with regard to accessing needed financial services. Despite these challenges, steps can be taken to improve understanding and utilization of financial services, and encourage homeownership.

Issues for Multilingual and Multicultural Populations

1. Promoting Participation in the Financial Services Process through Increased Understanding of the System

Because financial issues and education vary across cultures, acquiring an understanding of these differences is critical to increasing the role of minority markets in areas such as transaction accounts and homeownership. For some, there is a lack of trust of banks and government agencies. Others have varying attitudes toward spending and saving, and may use intra-cultural financial mechanisms such as peer lending and investing groups within their communities. Still others must adhere to religious restrictions, such as the Islamic prohibition on the payment of interest.

Moving beyond these differences also requires overcoming language and cultural barriers when delivering financial education and financial services. Through careful research and innovative programs, sectors can better understand the needs of minority/ethnic communities while promoting greater consumer knowledge of financial services and consumer protection rights.

To gain an improved understanding of financial service offerings, many consumers look to groups with which they are familiar and trust. Through partnerships with key organizations and institutions — including employers, consulates, religious leaders/houses of worship, community groups, community colleges, and schools — public education efforts can develop strategies to work effectively with minority markets.

Successful educational strategies should be consistent with cultural priorities and norms, and offer a range of activities, including inter-generational classes, youth-focused education, and family-based learning. By gaining trust in mainstream financial service providers, consumers, for instance, can learn the differences between banks, credit unions, and other financial service providers and understand how to shop for financial products and services.

Programs such as the FDIC's *New Alliance Task Force (NATF)*, DOL's *Las Mujeres y el Dinero*, a credit education and financial counseling agency targeted to serve immigrants, and a Texas credit union targeted to serve government employees, demonstrate how building strategic partnerships can empower communities in need to deliver successfully a wide range of linguistically and culturally responsive financial services and education programs.

FDIC's New Alliance Task Force Helps Hispanics Access Financial Services

To equip the Hispanic population with specific, understandable information on the benefits and importance of holding financial accounts, the credit process, and mainstream banking, the FDIC's *NATF* brings together public and private sector organizations to help increase the number of Hispanics in the financial system.[90] FDIC's *NATF* is a broad based coalition of banks, community based organizations, and others, providing Hispanics with the necessary financial education and support services to improve their access to the formal banking system. For example, in FDIC's Chicago Region, the *NATF's Financial Education Working Group* educates Hispanics on the benefits and importance of establishing a financial account, the credit process, and mainstream banking as an alternative to the "fringe" banking system. Ten thousand Hispanics have participated in financial education classes and workshops. Fifteen *NATF* banks in the Midwest are now offering products with remittance services that allow Hispanics to open bank accounts, avoid high-cost wire services, and incur lower remittance costs for sending money back home.[91] During 2003 and 2004, 50,000 new accounts totaling \$100 million (with an average account balance of \$2,000) were opened at NATF banks in the Midwest.[92]

U.S. Department of Labor's *Las Mujeres y el* Dinero Brings Financial Education to Hispanic Women

Between October 2003 and October 2004 the Women's Bureau of DOL sponsored Las *Mujeres y el Dinero* (Women and Money), a series of financial education conferences that targeted Hispanic women. The conferences, held in each of DOL's 10 regions, included motivational speakers and educational workshops. The conferences reached over 4,000 Hispanic women in Texas; Florida; Pennsylvania; Washington; Connecticut; Missouri; Ohio; Colorado; and New York.

Minnesota Counseling Agency Assists Muslims with Financial Issues

Through education and communication with local bankers and financial institutions, one credit education and financial counseling agency identifies resources able to assist Muslims in reaching their goals of purchasing homes, buying cars and owning businesses without violating their religious beliefs. Based in Minnesota, the agency has served more than 10,000 immigrants and refugees from the African community, helping them navigate the American financial system. Since 2000, the agency has provided a range of financial education on a variety of issues, including budgeting, banking, credit management, homebuying, investing, and tax filing. The agency also provides financial education to women through a center established to serve the economic development needs and to build the financial acumen of immigrant women.

Texas Credit Union Promotes Low-Cost Remittance Service

A Texas-based credit union targeted to government employees located on the United States-Mexico border serves a largely Hispanic membership. The credit union joined a major remittance network in October 2000 to offer members of the local community a safe alternative to more expensive wire transfer services. Remittance transactions are conducted in dedicated space within the credit union branch by bilingual employees who specialize in providing the service. For the credit union, the remittance service has helped build relationships and attracted underserved immigrants into the formal financial sector.

Summary

By working with leaders in multilingual and multicultural communities and building partnerships across public-private and private-private organizations, neighborhoods can ensure that cultural issues are properly addressed. Local leaders are particularly adept at identifying cultural norms, legal and government issues, information and product needs, effective delivery channels, and essential languages needed for successfully delivering financial education to minority markets. Through a commitment to increasing participation in mainstream financial services, community leaders are making an investment in the residents of their community.

2. Changing Perceptions about the Accessibility of Homeownership

Homeownership is an important part of financial security for all communities and markets. But for some, the process of buying and keeping a home is daunting. To better encourage homeownership in minority communities, education efforts should address language barriers and cultural influences, as well as possible misinformation. Through counseling, access to interpreters, homebuying and homeownership classes, and education programs offered in a variety of languages and at various cultural-specific venues, homeownership can become a reality for those in minority markets.

To help overcome the language barriers that may keep potential homeowners from fulfilling their dreams, initiatives such as a Midwestern homeownership resource center have successfully provided homeownership information and guidance in the languages needed by local residents.

Homeownership Center Employs Multilingual Resources to Promote Homeownership in Minnesota

Through native language classes and materials, more and more minority sector consumers in two cities in Minnesota are learning how to make homeownership a reality. The center provides dedicated interpreting services to consumers in need.[93] To assist English language learners, housing providers are able to tap the center's cadre of interpreters, all trained in homeownership essentials and financial terminology. The center offers homebuyer education classes for area residents in Spanish, Cambodian, Russian, and Hmong. Additionally, the center works in partnership with a wide range of private and public sector organizations and the two cities of Minnesota where, together, they are working to improve and standardize financial education efforts for minority populations while supporting high-quality counseling.

Summary

To increase homeownership in minority markets, local communities must work together to create and distribute home-buying materials and services in native languages.

3. Improving Access to Financial Services

Minority markets also face a number of obstacles to financial services, including physical proximity. In some communities, such as Native American reservations and ethnically concentrated neighborhoods, there may not be an abundance of financial institutions. These communities seek specific strategies to help them better secure the financial services resources, while gaining the products, underwriting, and delivery mechanisms that are culturally compatible.

In minority markets, successful financial behaviors are more likely to occur when citizens gain an increased knowledge and understanding of financial issues, and are provided the physical access to those services that are most beneficial.

By working through the public school system, English language providers, citizenship education centers, recreation organizations, and tax preparation sites, public and private sector organizations can increase access to financial services for underserved communities. Efforts such as the President's *Financial Literacy Initiative* and a Native American financial literacy program have demonstrated what is possible through improved access.

President Bush's Financial Literacy Initiative

Understanding the need for greater financial literacy in America that incorporates a specialized focus on increasing Hispanic ownership of financial assets, on May 4, 2005, President George W. Bush called upon agencies to serve on the first national public-private partnership with the Hispanic community. The Commission, led by the Treasury Department, the FDIC, and the SBA, will work with Hispanic groups, business associations, and the private sector to reach populations that traditionally have lacked financial education resources. The FDIC conducted a major advertising campaign for promoting the use of the *Money Smart* curriculum and offering local classes through FDIC's regional network and Hispanic groups. The SBA will continue to create Web-based instruction on its Spanish site www.sba.gov/espanol/. The Treasury Department will work with the Commission to maintain the availability of Spanish language materials on MyMoney.gov and the 1-888-MyMoney hotline.

Coalition Creates and Implements Customized Program to Build Financial Skills in Native American Families

Created by a coalition of community groups and foundations, one program provides Native American families with specific lessons to develop personal financial skills while embracing native traditions and values. Through a specifically designed curriculum, Native Americans receive the information, guidance, and assistance they need to help improve their financial standing. As part of this effort, community members are offered a range of program modules, including *Building a Healthy Economy, Developing a Spending Plan, Working with Checking and Saving Accounts, Understanding Credit and Your Credit Reports,* and *How to Access Credit.* Educators also are provided an instructor's guide and participant workbooks to help Native American families strengthen their personal financial skills.

Summary

For geographically remote and underserved areas of the country, consumers need increased physical access to the banks and other financial services necessary for proper financial planning, saving, and investment.

CALL TO ACTION

Tactics Employed: Public Awareness, Targeting

9-1 Between the fourth quarter of 2006 and the fourth quarter of 2007, the Treasury Department will host a series of roundtables on financial education topics of special concern to specific communities. The goal of each roundtable will be to raise awareness of the important financial education topics within the specific community highlighted.

10. KINDERGARTEN – POSTSECONDARY FINANCIAL EDUCATION

Overview

"Like all learning, financial education is a process that should begin at an early age and continue throughout life. This cumulative process builds the skills necessary for making critical financial decisions that affect one's ability to attain the assets, such as education, property, and savings, that improve economic well-being."[94] While few would dispute former Federal Reserve Chairman Alan Greenspan's statement, the truth is that for many of America's youth, financial literacy is still not a reality.

Each year, young Americans spend roughly $150 billion, yet they do not have a strong understanding of basic financial concepts such as annual percentage rates, inflation, and interest.[95] According to a survey on personal financial literacy administered in 2004, high school seniors answered just more than 50 percent of the financial literacy questions correctly.[96] While this demonstrated an increased aptitude on the issues for the first time since 1997, 66 percent of high school seniors still failed the exam.[97]

The survey results indicate that those students who successfully answered survey questions had something in common. Those seniors who attended money management courses in high school fared better than those who did not. In schools that required financial literacy classes for all students, 55 percent of the financial literacy questions were answered correctly.[98] The percentage of correct survey responses on financial literacy topics dipped to 51 percent in schools that required financial education only for some high school students, and 53 percent where money management was taught to students as an elective course.[99]

The survey results also indicate that the majority of participants (58 percent) learn most of their money management skills at home.[100] By comparison, 20 percent said they learned such skills at school and 18 percent said they learned from personal experience[101]

Struggles with financial literacy are not limited to high school students. According to the Department of Education's National Center for Education Statistics, more students who dropped out of college cited financial reasons, rather than academic ones, for their decision.[102] While there are many financial reasons that might contribute to a student dropping out of school, one of the factors may be the college students' inability to plan and manage their finances in ways that enable them to meet the expenses of college.

Challenges

Data gathered by various organizations demonstrate real challenges in financial literacy among youth, particularly during their formal education years. Some of these challenges include finding room for financial education in the school day, the lack of teacher preparedness on the issue, and a lack of awareness of effective materials and curricula. While the K-12 environment is key to addressing the need for more financial education, non-school venues and college-level programs also offer promising options.

Issues in K–Postsecondary Financial Education

1. Finding Room for Financial Education in K-12 Curricula through Integration

While many educators now understand the importance of teaching students basic money skills, often tightly regimented course schedules do not allow for the development of a separate, new course to meet this newly recognized priority. Typically, established core curricula consume most of the school day, leaving educators with little time to help their students become financially literate.

It may appear that subjects like math, science, social studies, economics, history, family and consumer science, and english all compete with financial education for precious space in a school's curricula, and that adding financial education would necessitate dropping some other discipline. But just the opposite is true — integration of financial education into established curricula permits schools and educators to meet their obligations to teach required courses while simultaneously exposing students to valuable financial literacy lessons.

For example, second graders learning basic addition can use coins not only to understand the value of money, but also to begin practicing their arithmetic. Middle school students studying percentages in math class can be taught about the compounding of interest rates. High school freshmen studying the Great Depression in history class can learn about the rise of the modern banking system and the Social Security system. High school seniors in a family and consumer science course can learn about how credit works while receiving instruction on how to shop for major purchases like cars and homes. Not only does this save precious class time, but the integration of financial education into "real world" contexts also carries the potential to attract students' interest and facilitate their learning.

In schools across the United States, students benefit from the integration of financial education into core subjects. Nonprofit organizations and the Federal government have played a role in developing materials and curriculum, such as *Money Math: Lessons for Life*. Moreover, other organizations have developed classroom newspapers that enable educators to use the news and trends of the business world to convey meaningful lessons to students. Educators and policymakers can also use the guidance contained in the Treasury Department's *White Paper on Financial Education Integration* when designing their own models for bringing financial knowledge to their students.

Nonprofit Organization Uses Volunteer Executives and Specialized Materials to Integrate Free Enterprise Topics in the Classroom

Through the use of volunteers and rigorously tested materials, an international nonprofit organization committed to providing every child with a fundamental understanding of the free enterprise system, also supports teachers' efforts to integrate financial education into a wide variety of courses. These courses include economics, business, career development, consumer/home economics/family & consumer sciences, American history, geography, government, mathematics, and world history. Coordinating closely with the classroom teacher, trained volunteers offer a real-world perspective on financially literate behavior for students. Positioned as in-class or after-school role models, the volunteers usually come from the business sector and work to support teachers and reinforce teaching concepts through frequent, coordinated classroom visits over the course of an academic semester. Volunteers deliver programming that helps students understand the "economics of life." The organization's program kits include classroom materials, supplies, and corresponding student, volunteer, and teacher guides. Sponsored by local businesses and community groups, these programs are offered at no charge to schools.

The organization works to teach students to understand and appreciate the free enterprise system. Financial literacy elements are interwoven throughout all the courses, in grades K-12. Local offices of the organization coordinate programming to match each community's needs, reaching approximately 4 million students in 145 markets in the United States.

Treasury Department and Midwestern University Collaborate to Develop Money-Based Math Curriculum

In 2001, the U.S. Department of the Treasury, working with a university in the Midwest, developed *Money Math: Lessons for Life*, a curriculum that uses real-world personal financial scenarios to teach mathematical concepts and basic finance to students in grades seven through nine. The lessons emphasize the application of math in savings, taxes, balancing budgets and home improvement projects. The kit contains reproducible activity sheets for students and incorporates the use of spreadsheets. Developed to adhere to national math standards allow for easy integration, the curriculum is appropriate for any class such as family and consumer science or social studies, or after school programs designed to teach practical financial or math skills to students in grades seven through nine. For example, learning to calculate compound interest and understanding its mathematical significance, allows students to appreciate the cumulative benefits of regular saving. The curriculum is available free of charge in electronic and hard copy formats at www.publicdebt. treas.gov/mar/marmoneymath.htm.

Major Financial Publication Brings Business and Economic Lessons into High Schools through Classroom Edition Newspaper and Customized Curriculum

Some teachers integrate financial education into their classrooms through the use of a student version of a business oriented newspaper. This classroom newspaper has been in publication for 14 years and is delivered each month to more than 5,000 secondary schools and to an estimated audience of 750,000 students.

In addition to the monthly student newspaper, the classroom newspaper service includes a teacher's guide that contains worksheets and lesson plans to help teachers integrate the contents of the newspaper into their curricula. There are additional lessons and teaching resources available on their Web site. The program also includes a single copy of the daily newspaper which allows teachers to reinforce economic principles in the classroom newspaper with day-to-day developments from the business world. The monthly student newspaper which features specially selected articles from the daily newspaper has included topics such as *Who Deserves Healthcare? and House of Cards: The Risks and Rewards of America's Credit Culture*. The stories are intended to use the news and trends of the business world to convey meaningful lessons that students can practice everyday — in school, at home, and in their communities. The classroom newspaper is delivered each month with the support of subscribers, sponsors, and partners in the public and private sectors.

The Treasury Department White Paper — Integrating Financial Education into School Curricula

In October of 2002, the Treasury Department released a White Paper on integration of financial education into school curricula, as a result of a panel discussion hosted by the Treasury Department and the Department of Education.[103] The White Paper is available at www.treasury.gov/financialeducation. The panel consisted of key national youth education groups, and focused on the benefits of incorporating financial education into math and reading curricula within a standards-based educational system.

The report, entitled *Integrating Financial Education into School Curricula*, identified five access points for bringing financial education into schools. The access points are state standards for education, testing, textbooks, financial education materials, and teacher training. The White Paper can serve as a practical roadmap for policy makers, educators, and others interested in accomplishing the goal of integrating financial education into core math and reading curricula. It also includes a list of Web-based clearinghouses and other organizations that compile lists of financial resources that target school-age audiences.

Summary

The starting point for giving people a basic understanding of personal finance is youth financial education, and the best starting place to reach large numbers of young people with financial education is in schools. Teaching financial education in schools starts the process of preparing children to become competent consumers and managers of household wealth.

While some schools may opt for a stand-alone class, the inability to provide such a class should not prevent a school or an educator from exposing students to financial topics. Integrating financial education concepts as part of other subjects, such as math, social studies or family and consumer science, offers a creative method of arming students with lifelong financial skills. Such integration not only enhances the teaching of subjects such as reading and math, but also makes financial education less susceptible to elimination due to local school budget cuts or changes in course offerings.

2. Providing Teachers with Training and Support to Effectively Teach Financial Education Topics

Many teachers are not trained to teach financial topics. Financial literacy is not something they were taught in college or learned through professional development, and therefore, they may not feel comfortable or confident in their abilities to teach it to students. Some teachers may also question their own personal level of financial literacy, making it difficult for them to instruct authoritatively on the subject. The result is that a teacher may fully recognize his or her students' need for financial education, but simply may not be trained to meet it.

By raising the level of educators' knowledge and confidence in teaching financial literacy subjects in a range of academic settings (including public schools, private schools, and community-based courses), schools can boost the availability of financial education to students. Through teacher training programs, effective materials and resources, and appropriate curricula, the financial literacy of educators, and the students they teach, can improve.

Through innovative programs in both Wisconsin and West Virginia, teachers and community educators are improving their knowledge of financial literacy issues and becoming more confident financial education instructors.

Wisconsin Program Instructs Teachers on Financial Literacy Topics

A program in the state of Wisconsin provides teachers with the training and education necessary to become effective financial literacy instructors. The program provides the materials, curricula, and resources to enhance the self-sufficiency and financial literacy of educators and the thousands of K-12 students they teach. In partnership with a state coalition for financial literacy, this program offers a series of week-long teacher-training courses to educators. These classes—held during the summer on a college campus in Wisconsin—

provide instruction and resources on issues such as personal finance, economics, savings and investing, insurance, credit, and entrepreneurship.

The curriculum is delivered by a blend of business and academic professionals and has created a motivational and professional experience that equips educators with content, materials, and skills to teach and promote financial literacy in their classrooms and communities.

Personal Finance Training Provided to West Virginia Educators

In 2001, a personal finance training program began in West Virginia. The program helps teachers master financial literacy topics by offering free courses to state educators and up to three hours of graduate, undergraduate or professional development credit. Topics include credit and credit counseling, identity theft, investor education, and a variety of other issues. The training program was initiated by a state coalition for financial literacy, and represents a coalition of state agencies, private businesses and educational organizations with an interest in personal finance.

Summary

Teachers should seek out and take advantage of financial education training in their state or region. Schools can also partner with local banks, credit unions, or other financial institutions to provide financial literacy training to teachers.

3. Providing Teachers with Effective Financial Literacy Materials, Curricula, and Resources

Even given the time and willingness to incorporate financial education into the school environment, many teachers lack the resources and knowledge necessary to develop and successfully teach a financial education program to their students. Similarly, many parents may not feel adequately equipped to successfully instruct their children on financial issues. Many teachers and parents are unaware of the wealth of financial education information and materials already available to them for little or no cost.

An abundance of financial education curricula exists to meet the needs of virtually all U.S. students. Several organizations have established clearinghouses of free or low-cost materials that can be used by educators and parents to teach financial concepts. State and local governments, businesses and nonprofit can all benefit from such materials they seek to implement financial education programs in their communities.

To better equip educators with available resources, schools can partner with organizations that develop, sponsor, and deliver financial education programs. Public-private and private-private partnerships can be successful in bringing financial education into the classrooms and equipping schools with the expertise and resources needed to teach valuable concepts.

Educators and families can access the financial education information and resources available in the marketplace through efforts from a national coalition for financial literacy and through a special clearinghouse for financial education.

National Coalition Maintains a Database of Financial Education Materials

A coalition for financial literacy seeks to help educators and parents, including parents of home schooled children, locate personal financial education materials.

To accomplish this, the coalition established a database of personal finance resources available from a variety of education providers, such as government, business and non-profit organizations.

This database is located on the coalition's Web site, and many of the materials are low cost or free of charge. Teachers can use these personal finance teaching materials to support their state's standards in economics, business, math and family and consumer science. To ensure that disseminated materials adhere to high standards, the coalition uses a review checklist as a guide in the selection of materials to be included in the database.

Foundation Provides Clearinghouse for Financial Education Materials

Educators throughout the nation, including parents of home schooled children, can turn to a Web-based clearinghouse for financial education to provide materials and curricula on a range of issues. The clearinghouse has materials for all ages, but has a particularly deep offering for young people, especially those in high school. The materials provided through the clearinghouse are sorted into subject areas on a variety of financial topics. Organizations can access teacher guides and classroom materials on financial education through the clearinghouse Web site.

Summary

Teachers and parents can draw on the wealth of free and low-cost materials available from the many organizations committed to the development and implementation of financial education curricula.

4. Increasing Financial Literacy by Reaching Youth in Non-Traditional Educational Venues

Teaching financial literacy is not a task to be addressed solely in schools. Non-profit organizations, private firms, youth clubs, and other youth organizations should be active and involved in providing resources and education to students throughout the nation. To complement what is happening in the classroom, involved organizations can reach out to youth through non-traditional methods and venues, offering tailored information that speaks directly to young people.

Through community education efforts such as those available through after- school programs, summer camps, personal finance clubs, correctional facilities, and youth service organizations, students are able to gain financial literacy skills through a non-school based environment. For example, students who have dropped out of high school are learning financial skills through an alternative high school in Arizona.

National Organization for Girls Teaches Financial Skills

A national organization for girls that teaches leadership, character and a variety of practical skills has also been teaching its members about financial literacy. The organization has developed a curriculum kit to help members ages nine to 11 increase their financial skills. The projects and activities included in the curriculum offer opportunities for volunteers to help girls learn, and put into action key concepts and skills related to personal money management.

The program also makes effective use of corporate partnerships to help educate their members. Working with various private companies, the program leaders developed Web sites specifically designed for young girls. Through these sites the girls learn about financial issues that they will face throughout different stages of their lives. These sites are tailored for and appeal to this particular demographic; for example, one site provides a video game where girls can pick a character and make its financial decisions in hopes of reaching established goals. The site also provides links to financial aid and scholarship opportunities.

The program also uses awards and badges to encourage financial literacy. These awards are received after members complete various tasks such as coming up with marketing campaigns to sell products or after completing certain exercises on the financial Web sites.

North Carolina Summer Camp Provides Financial Training as Essential Life Skill

In North Carolina, a summer camp teaches life skills to boys and girls from low-income homes entering the sixth, seventh or eighth grades. It is focused on combating a variety of problems, including a lack of financial education. Students who have demonstrated academic achievement and advancement over the previous school year are chosen from each county to participate in the program.

The camp activities focus on preparing middle school students for the day they begin their careers through classes in such topics as entrepreneurship, citizenship responsibilities, and conflict resolution, as well as business and banking. The students learn how to balance a checkbook, prepare a budget, make a profit in business, assess the value of money, and to manage money wisely. Campers also participate in traditional camp activities such as horseback riding, swimming and hiking.

National Network of After School Youth Centers Adopts Financial Education Curriculum

An after-school youth organization with community centers across the country has identified financial education as a priority for the young people it serves. This private-private partnership between a large discount brokerage house and a boys and girls club is committed to reaching young people and increasing their financial skills. Through their joint program, 4 million young people have access to additional financial education through a national network of 3,700 neighborhood-based facilities.

The organization primarily serves disadvantaged youth. In one major city in Colorado, for instance, 70 percent of the youth come from such households. The young people who are part of the financial literacy program receive personal financial education lessons, and gain new insight on issues like budgeting, saving, and investing. Teens from age 13 to 18 learn practical ways to save, spend and invest the money they earn. These lessons are taught by employees of this brokerage house who are given the time to volunteer and share their financial expertise with teenage club members and their families.

To date, more than 450 clubs have adopted the program, with approximately 36,000 teens expected to complete the program over the next two years. The club was able to initiate such a broad effort quickly because it partnered with a national brokerage firm that provided the financial education curriculum.

Minnesota Correctional Facility Recognizes Importance of Financial Skills in Rehabilitating Offenders

One of Minnesota's state correctional facilities is designed to provide treatment, education and transition services for serious and chronic male juvenile offenders. The average age of residents is just under 18. The facility's leadership considers deficiencies in financial management and related skills as risk factors for the youthful offenders being admitted to their facility. In response, the facility provides residents with the opportunity to learn financial and related skills in an effort to reduce the rate of recidivism. The program's goal is to equip residents to become successful members of society. Residents who have earned a high school diploma or GED participate in a program that provides instruction in the areas of financial management, independent living, and employment retention.

Participants in the facility's *Transition Services Program* participants scored in the top 8 percent nationwide among correctional programs studied under the *Corrections Program Assessment Inventory* (CPAI). CPAI is based on best practices and is the recommended assessment tool by the U.S. Department of Justice's National Institute of Corrections.

Youth Service Organization

A youth service organization offered by the Cooperative Extension System in partnership with USDA-CSREES, plays an important role in educating youth about money. The organization reaches 7 million young Americans annually, and has three national curricula to help young people understand the basics of earning and managing money so they can develop sound financial habits at an early age.[104]

In one of the programs, the youth service organization works with students to set financial goals, understand credit, and learn about financial planning. Another program helps youth become informed and responsible consumers in today's dynamic marketplace. A third program is an entrepreneurship effort focused on the knowledge, skills, and mindsets youth need to meet the pending challenges of work and community in the 21st century.

Alternative High School in Arizona Stresses Financial Knowledge for Students

Recent high school dropouts are learning about financial skills through a collaborative effort. Established through a partnership between the local school district and two foundations, this alternative public high school is designed to help those students (ages 17-21) who have dropped out of high school and who wish to earn a full diploma instead of a GED.

The students receive financial education training, obtain work experience, and participate in community service activities. They also learn through career development activities such as job shadowing, guest speakers, and workplace and college tours. The school offers its computer-based instruction through flexible, student-determined hours, while providing student counseling through a Career Resource Coordinator. The financial education curriculum and instruction is provided by the local credit union.

Summary

Through nonprofit organizations, private firms, youth clubs, and other youth organizations, students can receive much- needed financial literacy instruction. Designed to complement any financial instruction occurring in the schools, community-based education can reach out to youth through non-traditional methods. Others wishing to give students financial skills outside of the classroom can follow the example of the referenced programs and make use of non-traditional venues to reach youth on this important topic.

5. Increasing the Financial Skills of Postsecondary Students

According to the Department of Education's National Center for Education Statistics, among 9,000 students surveyed from 800 postsecondary institutions, approximately 3,300 did not successfully complete the program in which they were enrolled.[105] Nationally, 14 percent of students who left college without completing a degree cited financial reasons, while only 2 percent cited academic ones.

For these students who are facing financial difficulties, both in college and following, financial literacy skills can be a useful tool in navigating personal economic issues and succeeding in one's goals. These skills can be gained through financial education efforts offered through colleges, universities, lenders, and non-profit organizations.

The higher education institutions described below are providing financial literacy opportunities to students.

Florida Community College Teaches Personal Finance Topics

Under the guidance of faculty members from the School of Business and English as a Second Language Department, instructors from the college's five campuses have incorporated the financial education curriculum into their learning objectives.

Through a partnership with a large financial institution, the FDIC *Money Smart* curriculum is being delivered to students. Sessions are facilitated by students from business classes or by students in campus business organizations with a banking representative on hand to address specific bank product and service related questions.

The classes are open to the public, but primarily are marketed to the college's students. The college trained 380 participants in 2004 and over 1,000 students during the Spring 2005 semester. In 2005-2006, the college plans to expand the program and add a computer-based instruction option to reach even more students and community members.

University in Rhode Island Provides Incoming Students with Money Management Tools

At one Rhode Island university, incoming freshmen enroll in an online credit education course as part of freshman orientation. The program serves as a tutorial, providing an introduction to money management and credit use. This five-section program uses tailored materials such as worksheets to reinforce the concepts presented during each module.

Interested students can also enroll in a certificate program in Family Financial Counseling and Planning (FFCP) through the university's Department of Human Development and Family Studies. FFCP certificate holders can then use their financial literacy skills to find careers in personal financial counseling or planning on behalf of community organizations that serve families and children.

Summary

The years immediately following high school offer significant financial milestones for many. Successfully managing tuition and student loan needs, a first credit card, or a first apartment lease requires strong financial skills and access to the right information. To better equip postsecondary students with the money skills they need, colleges, universities, lenders, and non-profit organizations can play a crucial role in making financial education available to young people.

CALLS TO ACTION

Tactics Employed: Partnerships, Integration/Teachable Moments, Quality Materials

10-1 In 2006, the Treasury Department will partner with the U.S. Department of Education to host a summit focused on integration of financial education into the core school curriculum. The group also will survey promising practices in financial education and in teacher-training in an effort to assist others who are starting or enhancing programs. This public meeting will bring together policymakers, educators, and other leaders in the fields of general education and financial literacy. Findings from this summit will be made available to educators and policymakers throughout the nation.

10-2 Teachers, parents, and youth organizations should make greater use of the wealth of free and low-cost materials available on a variety of financial education topics through national clearing houses.

10-3 Postsecondary institutions should consider ways to raise the financial literacy levels of their students to help them avoid financial hardship due to mismanagement of credit and money.

11. ACADEMIC RESEARCH AND PROGRAM EVALUATION

Overview

Research has shown that many Americans lack knowledge of the basic personal economics they need to make informed financial judgments and manage their money effectively.[106] Across all demographic and age groups, Americans lack sufficient knowledge of personal finance issues. Research has affirmed this conclusion, and it is on this basis that greater attention is now being paid to promoting and expanding financial literacy efforts. Since the mid-1990s, many organizations have initiated financial literacy programs in response to this issue.[107] In fact, a recent study of financial literacy programs found that 65 percent of surveyed programs began in the 1990s, and almost 75 percent surveyed began in the late 1990s or early 2000.[108]

Since many financial literacy programs are relatively new, a common, systematic approach to developing and delivering financial education is still lacking. As schools, employers, community-based organizations, and Federal, state, and local, governments all work to help Americans achieve financial literacy, more research and program evaluation needs to be conducted so that organizations are able to validate or improve their efforts and measure the impact of their work on financial literacy levels.

Successful programs use testing, surveys, or other objective evaluation measures to prove their worth by demonstrating a positive impact on participants' attitudes, knowledge, or behavior, with formal program evaluation determining quality, effectiveness, or value. As individual financial education programs are deemed successful, these will help establish specific program goals and performance measures to track the progress and success of other programs, serving as models for future efforts.

Challenges

To properly evaluate financial literacy programs and move successful models into increased practice throughout the United States, financial education leaders can turn to both academic research and programs to help identify best practices.

Issues in Academic Research and Program Evaluation

1. Encouraging Academic Research

Research on the effectiveness of financial literacy programs has been conducted in a variety of areas, including credit, homeownership, savings, and retirement savings. Additionally, some studies have focused on the setting in which financial education has been provided, such as in the workplace or as part of high school curricula.

Samples of academic research conducted in the area of financial literacy and education include studies by the Credit Research Center at Georgetown University, the Pension Research Council at the Wharton School of the University of Pennsylvania, and the Center for Social Development at Washington University in St. Louis. Other areas of academic research include financial education in the workplace and in school curricula.

Credit Research Center at Georgetown University

Research conducted by the Credit Research Center at Georgetown University compared the usage of credit cards by three different groups — those opened by young adults through college student marketing programs; those opened through conventional marketing channels by young adults (aged 18-24); and those opened through conventional channels by older adults.[109] They found that student- marketed accounts had smaller balances, lower credit limits, and lower utilization rates than accounts opened by other groups. They also found that while student-marketed accounts were more likely to be delinquent and have a higher likelihood of charge-off, both the delinquency and charge-off rates of the student-marketed accounts and conventional accounts of young adults converged within 24 months.

The findings are consistent with credit card issuers' statements that they establish student accounts with relatively low credit limits, expecting that the large majority of new, young cardholders will learn how to manage a credit card, establish strong credit histories, and become longer-term credit customers.

Pension Research Council

Research at the Wharton School of the University of Pennsylvania examined a series of issues related to financial education using an annual survey of households conducted by a financial management and advisory company.[110] This research found that households fail to fully appreciate their financial vulnerabilities and do not posses adequate decision-making skills when it comes to financial matters. In light of this evidence, the research examines financial education programs offered through the workplace and focuses on the effects of these programs on household behaviors.

The study found that financial education in the workplace increases both the participation in private pension plans and the level of contributions to those plans. Thus, the study concludes that any improvements to financial education programs in the workplace would go a long way toward encouraging greater retirement savings.

Center for Social Development at Washington University in St. Louis

Studies from the Center for Social Development at Washington University in St. Louis have examined data from participants in the American Dream Policy Demonstration, a national demonstration of Individual Development Accounts (IDA).[111] The key difference between IDAs and other subsidized savings programs is that IDAs require financial education, and thus the population of participants is particularly of interest in the financial literacy arena. These studies from the Center for Social Development, the first quantitative look at the effects of financial education on savings in IDAs, found that 12 hours of general financial education increases savings, although the effects may diminish or reverse as hours increase.

Although the implications from these studies may only be drawn for participants in the American Dream Policy Demonstrations, the findings suggest that financial education has significant effects on savings behaviors, and that the courses do not need to be long to realize these positive effects. Moreover, the findings suggest that targeted, culturally-relevant marketing messages help convince people to attend financial education classes and to consider these classes to be worthwhile.

Financial Education in the Workplace

A number of studies have examined financial education in the workplace. Research conducted at Iowa State University examined the link between financial education in the workplace and workplace satisfaction.[112] Using data from a national sample of employees of an insurance company, the study found that employees who participate in workplace financial education more fully understand personal finances and recognize how financial literacy impacts their financial futures. Moreover, the study found that employees gain confidence in financial matters and their future financial situation through workplace education, and are more likely to be satisfied with and supportive of their company.

In addition, research conducted by the College of Management at North Carolina State University examined whether financial education programs effectively alter retirement savings goals and choices, such as contribution rates, income needs in retirement, and selection of retirement options in the pension plan.[113] Using data from three surveys of participants in a financial education seminar, they found that participation in the seminar increased contributions to pension plans and that many participants re-evaluated their expected retirement age and retirement income goals. However, the study also found that there was a substantial disconnect between the stated intention to change saving behavior and the actual actions taken by participants. For example, over one-third of participants reported that they simply failed to take the necessary steps to increase their retirement savings, despite the stated desire to do so after the program.

Research conducted for the National Bureau of Economic Research also examined the effects of financial education in the workplace.[114] Using a survey of households, this study looked at the effects of financial education programs offered in the workplace on general saving and on retirement saving. This research found that a significant number of employees rely heavily on financial education in the workplace, and that workplace financial education replaced other potentially authoritative sources, such as financial planners, and displaced other sources, such as parents and friends. The study also found that financial education in the workplace increased the rates of general saving and retirement saving.

Financial Education in School Curricula

Studies of financial education have also focused on its effects on students when financial education is taught through school curricula.[115] For instance, research from the National Bureau of Economic Research examined the long-term effects of high school curriculum mandates on adult decisions regarding savings. Using a survey of American households, the study found that state mandates that require high school students to receive instruction on topics related to household financial decisions (such as budgeting, credit management, savings, and investments) significantly increased asset accumulation once the students reached adulthood. These effects on asset accumulation were gradual over time rather than immediate.

Summary

Academic research on financial education and its effects on personal behavior is necessary to assist policy makers and program developers in the design and implementation of financial education programs.

2. Program Evaluation Utilizing Proven Quantitative Analysis

As financial literacy programs are implemented in communities throughout the nation, specific emphasis should be placed on making certain that materials and curricula are proven to be effective in improving financial literacy skills. By scientifically reviewing past performance and achievements, financial literacy providers can establish a clear sense of programmatic best practices and successes.

To effectively assess financial literacy programs, evaluators should ensure that: 1) materials are tested before publication under conditions that realistically replicate the target settings and audiences; 2) feedback from teachers and learners is collected and used to shape development and revision of materials; 3) materials include assessment tools, such as pre- and post-tests, and examples of acceptable work, where appropriate; and 4) assessment tools measure both student knowledge and behavioral change as a result of teaching and learning.

Both nonprofit and Federal sectors have evaluated their programs using quantitative methods. Organizations that developed such programs as a financial planning program for high school students, K-12 personal finance curriculum, and *Money Smart* have used empirical studies to evaluate the quality and delivery of their financial literacy education efforts.

Money Management Program Increases High School Students' Knowledge

Research demonstrates that high school students enrolled in a national nonprofit foundation's financial planning program are more skilled and confident with financial literacy issues. By conducting an extensive study of program participants, the foundation was able to empirically determine that high school students enrolled in the financial planning program nationwide know more about managing money and have begun using money management skills that will be with them for a lifetime. The financial planning program is offered in partnership with the and participating Land Grant University Cooperative Extension Services and associations of credit unions.

Available at no cost to all U.S. high schools, the financial planning program uses contemporary materials to teach the basics of personal finance to young people while developing life-long habits and attitudes about money. The study found that as a result of participation in the program, 60 percent of participants had changed their saving patterns. Of those who reported having changed their saving habits, 80 percent said they now save for what they really need or want and 20 percent indicated that they now save every time they receive money. Comparing financial knowledge and behaviors after participating in the curriculum to levels before the program began, 38 percent of students had improved skills for tracking spending, 61 percent knew more about the cost of credit, 58 percent improved their knowledge about investments, and 44 percent felt more confident about managing their money.

Students were surveyed before they studied the curriculum material, immediately after they completed the classes, and, again, three months after completion. Immediately after studying curriculum material, there was a statistically significant increase on all financial knowledge, behavior, and confidence questions. Three months after completion, students had statistical increases on all but one question. The nationwide, 18-month evaluation project was conducted by Minnesota Cooperative Extension in partnership with USDA CSREES.

Non-profit Documents Gains in Students' Financial Aptitude after Completion of Class

A personal finance curriculum developed by a non-profit organization focused on teaching young children about the free enterprise system. Detailed studies of the impact of this sequential and integrated program have spotlighted the organization's ability to improve financial skills among K-12 students. Students address business, economics, and finance issues by using information, applying basic skills, thinking critically, and solving complex problems. In studies of these programs by external evaluators, these students demonstrated a significant understanding of economics and business knowledge and an enhanced desire to stay in school and pursue a career in business.

Quantitative research on this personal finance curriculum demonstrated high levels of student interest in and understanding of financial issues and strong support from teachers and volunteers. Students not only made gains in their understanding of economic and business concepts, but they were able to use this understanding to make financially responsible decisions.

Overall the study found that students who had previously participated in the program had significantly more knowledge prior to beginning the program than students who had not previously participated.

Money Smart

The FDIC and a national nonprofit housing organization have partnered to conduct a survey of *Money Smart* students and the impact *Money Smart* has on participants' lives. In particular, the survey is attempting to determine if participants develop banking relationships, such as opening checking or savings accounts, obtaining loans or using other bank services, as a result of applying information learned from the *Money Smart* training. FDIC will survey students who have participated in *Money Smart* classes — specifically those classes focusing on basic banking, budgeting and financial management, and credit, including understanding the importance of a good credit report.

The survey will consist of conducting two questionnaires that *Money Smart* students complete and then a follow-up telephone interview six to twelve months after students complete their *Money Smart* training. The goal of the survey is to determine the extent to which *Money Smart* financial education training is effective in helping participants change their behavior to improve their money management skills.

Summary

A broad and deep base of research on financial education will assist policymakers and public and private sector providers of financial education in their work on financial literacy. While research has been conducted on financial literacy, some questions remain unanswered. Additionally, some practitioners of financial education may not be aware of the latest research on this subject.

3. Program Evaluation Utilizing Qualitative Evaluation

To supplement the quantitative research that highlights successful financial literacy efforts, educators, state and local governments, nonprofit organizations, and employers can also use qualitative measures to gauge the success of financial education programs.

To ensure that Americans have access to financial education programs that can assist them in obtaining the practical knowledge and skills necessary to make informed financial choices throughout their lives, the Treasury Department's Office of Financial Education (OFE) has published a list of eight elements of a successful financial education program. These eight indicators relate to program content, delivery, impact, and sustainability. Viewed collectively, the eight indicators serve as a guide for developing new programs or enhancing existing program strategies for achieving the greatest impact.

Indicator One: Focus on Basic Tenets

A successful financial education program should focus on one or more of the four basic tenets of financial empowerment— basic savings, credit management, home ownership, and retirement planning. While there are other worthwhile financial education topics, these four areas are the basic building blocks to achieving financial security.

Indicator Two: Tailored to Target Audience

A successful financial education program should be tailored to its target audience, taking into account the audience's language, culture, age, and experience. Cultural biases, language differences, and other related factors play an important role in the development of any educational program.

Indicator Three: Local Distribution

A successful financial education program has the most profound impact when it is delivered through a local distribution channel that makes effective use of community resources and contacts. Partnerships with local organizations that are already ingrained in the community are one of the most effective means of garnering support and acceptance within a community and will result in more efficient delivery of information.

Indicator Four: Participant Follow Up

A successful financial education program follows up with participants to reinforce the message and ensures that participants are able to apply the skills taught. These actions serve to further break down those barriers and pave the road to better access to financial services.

Indicator Five: Specific Program Goals

A successful financial education program establishes specific program goals and uses performance measures to track progress toward meeting those goals. To achieve goals, an organization must first set goals. It is important that financial education providers set a standard of excellence and track progress toward achieving their missions.

Indicator Six: Demonstrable Impact

A successful financial education program can prove its worth by demonstrating a positive impact on participants' attitudes, knowledge, or behavior through testing, surveying, and other objective evaluation. Programmatic success — both for the individual and the community — can be measured, for instance, by determining if participants increased savings, opened bank accounts, saved for a home, or qualified for a mortgage at higher rates than nonprogram participants.

Indicator Seven: Replicability

A successful financial education program can be easily replicated on a local, regional, or national basis so as to have broad impact and sustainability.

Indicator Eight: Built to Last

A successful financial education program is built to last as evidenced by factors such as continuing financial support, legislative backing, or integration into an established course of instruction. This element simply recognizes that good programs must have the ability to survive if they are to have a strong impact.

In practice, these indicators have been put to use to recognize programs, such as those honored with the John Sherman Award for Excellence in Financial Education, that are making a difference in financial literacy.

John Sherman Award for Excellence in Financial Education

Through its John Sherman Award, the Treasury Department honors programs that embody the qualitative achievements identified in its Eight Indicators. The award is named for John Sherman, the 32nd Secretary of the Treasury who served from 1877 to 1881 in the administration of President Rutherford B. Hayes. Established by the Treasury Department's OFE, the John Sherman Award for Excellence in Financial Education recognizes organizations around the country with exemplary financial education programs.

By raising public awareness of effective financial education practices, the John Sherman Award serves two purposes. First, it honors successful programs, which helps increase participation by individuals in the community and also raises the program's stature in ways which may help with fundraising. Second, it provides others with model programs to assist with the development of initiatives in communities that need financial literacy assistance.

The award's Web site, which includes a list of past recipients, is located at www. treas.gov/offices/domestic-finance/ financial-institution/fin-education/.

Summary

Effective programs possess similar characteristics. Successful programs not only produce positive statistical results, but also embody qualities that reflect program focus, focus on intended audiences, and a commitment to public outreach. Such programs also set specific goals and demonstrate replicable results. The eight specific indicators developed by the Treasury Department are resources that can help key decision makers determine the effectiveness of the financial literacy methods they are using.

Call to Action

Tactics Employed: Public Awareness, Quality Materials

11-1 The Treasury Department along with the Department of Agriculture Cooperative State Research, Education, and Extension Service, will convene a symposium of researchers who specialize in financial education between the third quarter of 2006 and the third quarter of 2007. The goal of the symposium is to raise awareness of existing academic research and to define questions that require additional analysis. The symposium will result in a White Paper that will survey current financial education research and will also identify areas of potential future research.

12. Coordination Efforts

Overview

Fulfilling its mission under section 114 of Title V of the FACT Act, the Treasury Department, with significant input from the Commission, has worked to analyze existing financial education resources, particularly publications and programs, in an effort to "identify areas of overlap and duplication among Federal financial literacy and education programs, and develop a plan to improve the coordination of such activities."

To lead the Commission in its duties, the Treasury Department's Office of Financial Education (OFE) was designated by Congress to lend its expertise and provide primary support to the Commission. OFE was established in May 2002 as part of the Treasury Department's long-term commitment to ensure that all Americans have access to financial education programs that will help them make informed financial decisions throughout their lives. As part of the commitment, the OFE has assumed primary responsibility on Commission initiatives, specifically in regards to My Money resources and other areas of coordination.

Issues in Coordination

1. Coordination of Federal Information on Financial Literacy

Each year, Federal agencies develop information and education materials on consumer finance and consumer protection issues. Much of this information is now made available through the World Wide Web, as Americans turn to Federal agencies' Web sites for immediate and dependable information on issues of concern.

To ensure that consumers are provided one central location for all up-to-date information on financial literacy, the Commission launched its My Money campaign. Through this effort, the Commission established a Web site, MyMoney.gov to serve as a central clearinghouse for all Federal financial literacy information and resources, and a toll-free hotline, 1-888-MyMoney, where citizens can obtain a free My Money Tool Kit of useful Federal publications.

My Money

Providing consumers with one-stop shopping for financial information, the Commission established the MyMoney.gov Web site, a central repository for all Federal financial and consumer education materials. Through MyMoney.gov, Americans are better equipped with important information on how to better manage their money, and thus improve their lives.

The Web site provides information on key consumer topics, including budgeting and taxes; credit; financial planning; homeownership; privacy, fraud, and scams; responding to life events; retirement planning; saving and investing; and starting a small business.

Through the online site, consumers can request the My Money Tool Kit, which provides information on personal financial management issues such as investing, managing credit wisely, planning for retirement, and understanding Social Security benefits. The tool kit also provides citizen access to a wider variety of personal financial information through the Consumer Information Catalog. The quarterly Catalog, produced by the GSA Federal Citizen Information Center (FCIC), lists more than 200 of the most popular and helpful publications produced by more than 40 Federal agencies, including Commission members.

The MyMoney.gov Web site was established through the Commission's Web Site Subcommittee. The site is hosted by the FCIC. Members of the subcommittee included representatives from the FRB, NCUA, and SEC, Department of Education, USDA, DoD, HHS and HUD, DOL, Treasury Department, VA, FTC, GSA, SBA, SSA, CFTC, and OPM.

In addition to the MyMoney.gov Web site, Americans can also call the 1-888-MyMoney hotline to order a free tool kit of useful Federal publications that will help them build financial literacy. Operators take orders in English and Spanish for tool kit publications. Many of the publications offered as part of the tool kit are available in English and Spanish and all *My Money* resources are available free of charge.

To help develop the hotline, the Commission established a hotline subcommittee, comprised of representatives from the OTS, FDIC, NCUA, HHS, Treasury Department, and GSA. The hotline operation is part of the GSA's National Contact Center.

Summary

To ensure that all consumers are able to receive accurate, up-to-date, and easy-to-find information and resources on financial skills, the Commission launched its My Money initiative. Through increased public awareness of the resources available through My Money, including a national public service announcement campaign, the Commission can provide Americans access to valuable Federal financial literacy programs, materials, and information.

2. Assessing Federal Resources and Avoiding Duplication and Redundancy

It is important for Federal agencies to ensure that available resources are effective, current and avoid redundancy and overlap.

American taxpayers deserve Federal financial literacy resources that are effective. To make sure the taxpayers have access to effective resources, the Commission tasked all of its members with evaluating their own financial literacy resources to determine their effectiveness. The Commission collected the agencies' self-reported evaluation data and presented the data in the Strategy for Assuring Financial Empowerment (*SAFE Strategy*) which will be updated and submitted to Congress annually. Each agency deemed its programs and resources to be effective and worthy of continuance.

The Commission reviewed Federal financial literacy and education programs and resources to identify possible overlap and duplication. After reviewing these programs and resources, the Commission found that some appeared to be the same on the surface. However, upon closer inspection, it became clear that the resources had important differences. The differences might have been in the target audience, the delivery platform or specific content.

For example, although there is an apparent overlap between the DOL's Web-based publication, *Preparation for Retirement, and the SSA's Step by Step Retirement Planner*, the two resources offer very different information. DOL's publication includes information on employer-provided pensions, profit-sharing plans, and tax- sheltered savings plans. In contrast, the SSA resource provides detailed information on Social Security benefits and requirements.

In many cases, two resources might have shared a small amount of similar information, because the information in each resource was prerequisite to discussing the main topic of the resource which was vastly different in each resource. In these instances the same basic concepts were communicated so that the consumer could better understand the different, more advanced concepts that followed. For instance, the FRB's publication, *How to Establish, Use, and Protect Your Credit*, provides similar information to that of multiple FTC Internet and print publications (i.e., *Credit Repair, Building a Better Credit Record, How to Dispute*

Credit Report Errors, and ID Theft). The main difference between these two agencies' materials is that the FTC's are more detailed than those of the FRB.

Finally, some resources may address the same topic but target different audiences. In these resources, the same concepts may be presented in greater or lesser specificity, depending upon the audience and its level of financial sophistication. For example, DOL's *Savings Fitness* and the SEC's *Tips for Teaching Students about Savings* provide general information about how to start saving. The SEC's online publication, however, targets teachers while DOL's publication is an overview for all Americans.

When considering how to reduce apparent duplication in various publications it is important not to lose the benefits that come from customizing a resource to its intended audience. Moreover, it is also important to avoid fragmenting the information so that consumers would have to search for and consult several documents for a complete answer to their financial questions on a particular topic.

After a review of Federal financial literacy materials, the Commission concluded that, to the degree overlap existed, it was both minimal and necessary.

The Commission is working with all of its members to ensure that Federal agencies work together and avoid "recreating the wheel" when it comes to producing financial literacy materials. In this way, the Federal government can get the most effective use from financial literacy resources by utilizing existing programs and publications, rather than expending additional funds to create new resources. For example, several Commission members create valuable programs and publications, affording other Commission members the ability to utilize these tools without creating their own new resources. This can be seen by looking at various examples such as the partnership with the DOL, the IRS and the SBA and the *Money Smart* program resources provided by the FDIC. By doing this, Commission members work together to avoid duplication and redundancy.

U.S. Department of Labor, Internal Revenue Service and the Small Business Administration

The DOL works in partnership with the IRS to develop publications regarding retirement plans that the SBA disseminates to various small business owners and employees. The DOL and IRS create publications about various types of retirement plans pertaining to small businesses, such as Simplified Employee Pension Plans (SEP), and Savings Incentive Match Plans for Employees (SIMPLE). Rather than recreating existing publications or developing new resources that highlight these types of retirement plans, the SBA utilizes the DOL's and IRS's existing resources and sends these publications out to small businesses seeking information on these types of retirement plans.

The Federal Deposit Insurance Corporation *Money Smart* Program

The FDIC's *Money Smart* program is another example of a Federal government program that reduces redundancy among Federal financial literacy resources. Rather than creating a similar program and developing similar teaching curricula, numerous Federal agencies including eight Commission members utilize the FDIC's *Money Smart* program. Specifically, DOL opted to utilize the *Money Smart* program at One Stop Career Centers established under the Workforce Investment Act. One Stop Career Centers offer *Money Smart* in coordination with programs targeted to populations that may be outside the financial mainstream, such as welfare-to-work participants, individuals with no access to mainstream financial service providers, public housing residents, immigrants and low-income homebuyers. There are One Stop Career Centers all across the country that use the *Money Smart* program.

Summary

The Commission will continually assess the Federal government financial education resources, and will make recommendations as to which programs and publications should be enhanced, updated, or discontinued. In addition, the Commission will encourage its members to utilize existing resources, rather than create their own.

CALLS TO ACTION

Tactic Employed: Public Awareness

12-1 The Financial Literacy and Education Commission will continue to enhance the Web site MyMoney.gov to make it more comprehensive and interactive. The Commission will also work with other organizations to promote the awareness and use of the Web site.

12-2 Every six months the GSA and the Treasury Department will partner to survey Federal financial literacy and education programs and resources to identify potential overlap and duplication. The results of this survey will be put in report form and will be submitted to Commission members, with the first report to be issued in September 2006.

13. INTERNATIONAL PERSPECTIVE

Overview

Since financial literacy impacts the global economy, concern for financial literacy expands beyond our shores. Just as in the United States, other nations with consumer markets seek to educate their citizens on issues such as credit, money management, and investment. Educators and financial planners in the United Kingdom, Australia, New Zealand, Japan, and other countries are dealing with issues parallel to those faced in the United States. In Australia for instance, a recent survey of adults suggested that workers could benefit from education about retirement planning.[116]

Countries with emerging consumer markets also are concentrating on the need to educate consumers on financial issues. As part of ongoing efforts to grow free market economies, emerging nations are focusing ongoing efforts to include financial literacy as part of their overall economic development strategies. Although not every international effort to increase financial education is mentioned, below are several valuable initiatives that highlight some of the great efforts to improve financial literacy around the globe.

Challenges

In the United States, those involved in financial education struggle with generating public awareness of the need for financial education and getting the right information to the right people at the right time. It is instructive to note that other nations are confronting the same issues. More valuable still is observing the ways other countries address these issues and which practices are proving most successful.

Issues in International Perspective

1. Approaches Within Other Nations and Cross-Border Efforts

Nations and regions are changing demographically each day. Increased diversity means new populations that require tailored communications and education. Countries are beginning to recognize this, and increasingly they see the need for all individuals in their populations to be better informed on financial matters. With this recognition, though, comes the reality that there are few available mechanisms to share lessons learned and to enact systematic improvements for educating and informing the public on financial issues.

Several nations appear to be developing parallel efforts to establish national level initiatives to improve financial literacy. Dialogue between the organizations responsible for these initiatives can validate activities and expand the range of best practices. By learning from similar countries and using international organizations to find solutions to common problems, organizations such as the Organization for Economic Co-operation and Development (OECD), International Organization of Securities Commissions (IOSCO), Counsel of Securities Regulators of the Americas (CSRA), an international securities association United Kingdom's financial services regulator, Japan's Central Council for Financial Services Information (the Central Council) and the Australian Securities and Investments Commission (ASIC) are identifying ways to enhance financial literacy efforts.

Organization for Economic Co-operation and Development

The OECD is comprised of 30 member countries with a commitment to democratic government and a market- based economy. The OECD has active relationships with some 70 other countries and other non-governmental organizations and is well known for its publications and its statistics. Its work spans economic and social issues including macroeconomics, trade, education, development, and science/innovation.

In late 2005, OECD released a report entitled *Thirty Principles and Good Practices for Financial Education and Awareness* that provided international guidance useful in improving financial education and awareness in OECD and non-OECD countries. The OECD report highlights the importance of financial education in terms of helping individuals budget and manage their income, save and invest efficiently, and avoid becoming victims of fraud. The report also stresses the need for financially educated individuals to focus on increasing knowledge of investment guidelines and consumer protection laws. The implementation of these voluntary guidelines and good practices will vary from country to country, taking into consideration the various economic, social, demographic, and cultural factors of different nations.

The International Organization of Securities Commissions

The IOSCO is an international organization with approximately 181 member regulators that together oversee more than 90 percent of the world's securities markets. The IOSCO and its member organizations work together to try to ensure fair, efficient, and sound regulation of the world's financial markets. One of the main focuses of IOSCO is to encourage the global objective of robust investor protection. The IOSCO and its member organizations recognize that to achieve the high levels of investor protection, they need to focus on promoting financial literacy across the globe. To this end, many individual IOSCO member organizations have created their own in-country investor education programs. These education initiatives include consumer publications, hotlines, Web sites, investor alerts, financial literacy curricula, town meetings, investing tools, and plain language disclosure documents.

Additionally, the IOSCO and its working committees have published several reports on global investor education efforts. One such report, published in 2002, focused on emerging market countries and indicated that 27 of 33 developing countries surveyed had some type of investor education initiative in place. The report noted that the main goals behind initiating investor education programs in these emerging market countries was to improve financial and investment literacy among local investors and to increase awareness of investors' rights and duties and public interest in market development and growth. This report demonstrates securities regulators' global concern for promoting financial literacy as part of their overall investor protection mission.

The Counsel of Securities Regulators of the Americas

The COSRA was founded in 1992 as an organization designed to provide a mutual forum for cooperation and communication amongst securities regulators in the Western Hemisphere. The COSRA currently includes more than 31 member organizations from 26 countries in North, South and Central America, as well as the Caribbean. Since its inception, the COSRA has focused on the need for strong investor education programs. The COSRA's focus on investor education comes from the recognition that widespread participation in financial markets is in the best interest of economic development.

In the 1990s, the COSRA developed an investor education and protection campaign designed to serve as a catalyst for its member organizations throughout the region. As early as 1998, the COSRA held an investor education week where each of its members conducted a domestic investor education campaign. Based on this campaign, a continuing annual effort was launched by member countries to provide education programs to investors in their respective countries. These programs have included town meetings, radio and television shows, seminars, brochures, public service announcements, and toll- free telephone numbers for investor questions and complaints. The COSRA campaigns strive to provide investors with information about the importance of investing, how to choose investments wisely, and the use of investment professionals.

International Securities Association Organization

An international securities association organization is composed of trade and self-regulatory associations in eleven countries and is a member organization that is aimed at encouraging growth of the international securities markets. This organization believes investor education is critical to the long term growth of the international securities markets. As such, one of its major policy initiatives is to focus on effective international investor education efforts. The organization's members believe that educated consumers who are able to make informed judgments regarding their investments are more apt to invest in securities products, promoting their own well-being, which will in turn contribute to the growth of securities markets, higher levels of savings, and a more efficient allocation of capital.

To demonstrate its commitment to investor education, the organization published a paper in 2004 that endorsed several principles and best practices focused on providing investor education. These principles focus on the need for broad, effective dissemination of comprehensive investor education programs by organizations in the securities industry. The organization also focuses on applying these investor education principles to enhance the continued growth of international securities markets. For example, members of the organization are currently working with the International Forum for Investor Education (IFIE). IFIE provides information on investment processes in the international financial market and on investor education programs in different parts of the world. In addition, IFIE provides the most up-to-date information on current trends in investor education through the dissemination of relevant research to its members.

Financial Services Regulatory Agency (United Kingdom)

The non-governmental financial services regulatory agency in the United Kingdom (UK) is an independent non-governmental body given statutory powers by the Financial Services and Markets Act 2000. Its overall aim is to promote efficient, orderly, and fair markets and to help retail consumers achieve a fair deal. The agency's primary focus is to regulate financial service providers in the UK, but it also has other statutory objectives, one of which is to promote public understanding of the financial system.

In November 2003 the agency proposed to develop and implement a national strategy for financial capability, working in partnership with a wide range of other organizations. The chief executive chairs a steering group comprising senior representatives of core partners—government, firms, employers, not- for-profit organizations, consumer representatives and the media. The agency recognizes that improving financial capability is complementary to, not a substitute for, firms treating their customers fairly. Consumer understanding and awareness influence both the nature and intensity of the regulation needed for consumer protection and whether consumers derive benefits from competition in the market place.

The Financial Capability Steering Group has identified seven priority projects: school, young adults, workplace, families, planning ahead for retirement, borrowing and the role of generic advice. Each of these priorities is being taken forward by a specially convened working group. Steps are being taken to enable the impact of the national strategy to be measured.

Central Council for Financial Services Information (Japan)

In Japan, financial services information activities are conducted by the Central Council for Financial Services Information. The Central Council's mission is to educate the public about the importance of basic financial and economic knowledge related to daily life. Since 1983 the Central Council has been engaged in the nationwide promotion of financial and economic knowledge and education through a variety of multi-media efforts, such as newspapers, videotapes, a Web site, a free computer consultation service, and a regular survey on household finances. In its outreach efforts, the Central Council launches multi-media campaigns to increase basic financial education knowledge, hosts life planning events, provides consulting services, and partners with government institutions, schools, families, and communities to conduct activities that strive to teach children the importance of a family budget and debt management. The Central Council is comprised of experts in financial services information and representatives of financial, industrial, communications, community and similar organizations.

Australian Securities and Investments Commission

The Australian Securities and Investments Commission (ASIC) has an active financial literacy program, and has established a national strategy as a part of its Consumer and Financial Literacy Task Force. To develop its strategy, the ASIC has conducted research on successful financial literacy models in the United Kingdom and the United States and has surveyed Australians on financial literacy issues. Through support from a major bank, the local survey has demonstrated that financial literacy among younger and older people requires specific attention. The ASIC is employing innovative approaches to reach these specific groups, such as a comic strip called *The Max*, targeted toward 14- to18- year-olds and designed to appeal to this age group.

2. Encouraging Global Partnerships

Given the global economy and the benefit of sharing knowledge at an international level, better communication and education among nations — particularly through partnerships — would allow for more rapid assimilation of improvements throughout the world.

Nations are working to establish comprehensive strategies to direct available government resources to educate consumers. Successful governmental approaches are emphasizing effective collaborations with non-profit and the private sector. Through partnerships with organizations like the worldwide representative of credit unions, a global non-profit organization that works with students, Asia-Pacific Financial Education Exchange, and Germany's Oeconomix, nations have added to their capacity to develop public awareness campaigns and financial educational materials, as well as deliver services to citizens who need them most.

Worldwide Representation of Credit Unions

The organization that provides worldwide representation for credit unions serves as a leading advocate and platform for knowledge exchange and functions as a development agency for credit unions. The organization also presents an opportunity to promote financial education in many countries. This organization represents the interests of more than 40,000 credit unions in 84 countries serving 123 million credit union member-clients. The organization currently carries out technical assistance programs in ten countries focused on improving financial performance, mobilizing savings and increasing outreach to create access to quality credit unions for everyone.

A United States national association of credit unions is the organization's largest member. U.S. credit unions are linked to credit union movements in developing nations through an international partnership. Fifteen U.S. credit union leagues have entered into partnership agreements, leveraging U.S. foreign aid by providing technical assistance and exchanging innovative approaches to serving credit union members with partner movements. The not-for-profit cooperative structure of credit unions is the same around the world, with "one member, one vote" guiding the election of board members, determining the future of the financial institution, and ultimately helping to create ownership societies.

Global Non-profit Organization Focused on Free Enterprise Spreads Financial Literacy Internationally

Financially focused students throughout the world are not limited by national boundaries as they work together on free enterprise issues. A global non-profit organization that works with students on 1,800 university campuses in more than 40 countries provides opportunities to learn about free enterprise. This organization helps students develop financial literacy skills and identifies opportunities for individuals to volunteer in their local communities by teaching personal finance, entrepreneurship, business ethics, and market economics.

International Foundation Creates Financial Education Resources on Two Continents

In Asia, a U.S. private sector foundation partnered with one of the world's top business schools, and hosted the women's financial education conference in Hong Kong. A key outcome of the conference was the idea to create an online knowledge and learning platform that will give local financial education providers greater access to training and resource materials, allowing them to share their knowledge and experience with more women as well as the wider community at a grassroots level.

In Germany, the same foundation is working with the Institute of German Economics to develop an innovative CD-ROM and Internet-based program which contains lesson plans, visual aids, and supplementary resources to help educators teach students about personal and family financial management, entrepreneurship, and corporate finance. In 2004, more than 650 teachers registered for the program.

CALL TO ACTION

Tactic Employed: Partnerships

13-1 Between the third quarter of 2006 and the second quarter of 2007, the Treasury Department will host an international summit on financial education. To bring about this multinational dialogue the Treasury Department will invite the central government authorities responsible for financial literacy in their respective nations to convene and discuss recent developments, innovative methods, and successful strategies for improving financial literacy in their home countries.

Across the world, nations are focusing additional attention and resources on financial literacy efforts. Through the cultivation of public-private partnerships like these, governments can help their citizens secure the necessary information and comfort level needed to access relevant financial services.

ACRONYMS

National Strategy for Financial Literacy Acronyms

APR	Annual Percentage Rate
ASIC	Australian Securities and Investment Commission
ATM	Automated Teller Machine
CFTC	Commodity Futures Trading Commission
COSRA	The Council of Securities Regulators of the Americas
CPA	Certified Public Accountants
CPAI	Corrections Program Assessment Inventory
CRA	Credit Reporting Agency
CSREES	Cooperative State Research, Education, and Extension Service
DOD	U.S. Department of Defense
DOL	U.S. Department of Labor
EITC	Earned Income Tax Credit
ESA	Education Savings Account
ETF	Mutual Fund and Exchange Traded Fund
FACT Act	Fair and Accurate Credit Transactions Act
FBI	Federal Bureau of Investigation
FCRA	Fair Credit Reporting Act
FDIC	Federal Deposit Insurance Corporation
FFCP	Family Financial Counseling and Planning
FHA	Federal Housing Administration
FHLB	Federal Home Loan Bank
FRB	Federal Reserve Board
FRTIB	Federal Retirement Thrift Investment Board
FSA	Financial Services Authority
FTC	Federal Trade Commission
GAO	U.S. Government Accountability Office
GED	General Educational Development
GSA	U.S. General Services Administration
HDHP	High Deductible Health Plan
HHS	U.S. Department of Health and Human Services
HAS	Health Savings Account
HSFPP	High School Financial Planning Program
HUD	U.S. Department of Housing and Urban Development
IDA	Individual Development Account
IFIE	International Forum for Investor Education

IOSCO	The International Organization of Securities Commissions
IRA	Individual Retirement Account
IRS	Internal Revenue Service
ITIN	Individual Tax Identification Number
LITC	Low-Income Taxpayer Clinic
NASD	National Association of Securities Dealers
NASAA	North American Securities Administrators Association
NCPW	National Consumer Protection Week
NCUA	National Credit Union Administration
OCC	Office of the Comptroller of the Currency
ODEP	Office of Disability Employment Policy
OECD	Organization for Economic Co-operation and Development
OFE	U.S. Department of the Treasury's Office of Financial Education
OPM	U.S. Office of Personnel Management
OTS	Office of the Thrift Supervision
PSA	Public Service Announcement
SAFE	Strategy for Ensuring Financial Empowerment
SBA	U.S. Small Business Administration
SEC	U.S. Securities and Exchange Commission
SEP	Simplified Employer Pension
SIMPLE	Savings Incentive Match Plan for Employees
SSA	Social Security Administration
SSDI	Social Security Disability Insurance
SSI	Supplemental Security Income
TAS	Taxpayer Advocate Service
TCE	IRS Tax Counseling for the Elderly Program
TSP	Thrift Savings Plan
USDA	U.S. Department of Agriculture
VITA	IRS Voluntary Income Tax Assistance Program
WISE	Winning through Investment Strategies and Education
WOTC	Work Opportunity Tax Credit

APPENDIX A. FINANCIAL LITERACY AND EDUCATION COMMISSION

Other Commercial Sector- Specific Meeting

Location:
Securities and Exchange Commission, 450 5th Street, NW, Washington, D.C.

Date:
February 25, 2005

Discussion Moderators

The discussion was moderated by Dan Iannicola, Treasury Department; John Nester, Securities and Exchange Commission; and Carolyn Welch, Federal Reserve Board.

Discussion Participants

DAN IANNICOLA, Treasury Department
JOHN NESTER, Securities and Exchange Commission
CAROLYN WELCH, Federal Reserve Board
SUSAN WYDERKO, Securities and Exchange Commission
MICHAEL BEACHAM, Money Savvy Generation
LAURA DAMBIER, Lincoln Financial Group
BILL DEERY, REMTECH, Inc./TimeMAPS
GENE FULLER, REMTECH, Inc./TimeMAPS
MICHELLE GLASSBURN, Eleve Group, Inc.
MARK GUIMOND, American Association of Debt Management
KATY JACOB, Center for Financial Services Innovation
CHRISTOPHER JACOBS, American Council of Life Insurers
JENNA KEEHNEN, U.S. Organizations for Bankruptcy Alternatives
MATHILDA RICHARDSON-WHITFIELD, AAA Straight Forward
ELINORE ROBEY, Charles Schwab Foundation
JOANNE SEYMOUR, Dynaminds, Inc.
AMY TRAVERSA, Lincoln Financial Group
CAROL WALKER, Financial Freedom, Inc.

Primary Focus of Meeting

Participants discussed the shared responsibility for better educating consumers on financial issues. Successful programs and initiatives require the involvement of both public- and private-sector organizations, with parties playing specific roles that emphasize their strengths in the dialogue. In addition to effective materials and financial education curricula, public awareness campaigns are a strong component of increasing consumer knowledge of financial issues and concerns.

Key Discussion Points

Role of Federal Government

Participants noted that the Federal government plays an appropriate and vital role in financial education efforts, particularly by focusing on efforts that emphasize the importance of financial education and place the topic on par, in terms of community concern, with issues such as nutrition, physical fitness and general health. To aid this effort, the Federal government should study the types of financial education programs and delivery mechanisms that are most effective and most needed. Research also could be used to establish uniform standards for financial education programs and to help highlight best practices as models for effective partnerships, materials development, delivery, and results measurement.

The Federal government also should catalogue existing financial education materials, oversee the development of new materials, and provide incentives for financial education program development and delivery. Specific legislative and policy changes also could be enacted to simplify financial transactions.

Effective Delivery Mechanisms

Participants identified the public school system as an important delivery channel for financial education, indicating that financial education efforts should be required, either as part of the current curricula (through integration of personal finance lessons) or as a specifically designated requirement for graduation. In addition to the schools, special emphasis should be placed on providing financially distressed families with information on credit counseling and debt management plans, working with community-based programs to reach children in "fun" environments, and using computer-based materials to reach those individuals who do not respond to group education.

Employers and family courts also are seen as valuable outlets for financial education and counseling, particularly if awareness programs are "turnkey" for easy use and integration by all organizations.

Materials and Curricula Development

There was no consensus on who should be primarily responsible for developing financial education resources. The public sector is an unbiased and credible source for information, but may be a better coordinator than originator. The private sector is a strong source of innovative and creative materials and programs. The primary source of the materials is not as important as ensuring that the materials are thoroughly and systematically distributed and adhere to a consistent set of standards. The point also was made that sales and marketing materials from private sector sources are not the same as true financial education materials.

Fundamental Financial Education Skills

Participants identified several skills that should be fostered in financial education efforts: 1) budgeting and saving; 2) shopping for financial products and services; 3) delaying gratification; 4) understanding credit cards; 5) setting financial goals throughout life; and 6) understanding options and resources available when confronted with financial difficulties such as debt negotiation, credit counseling and debt management plans.

Public Service Announcements and Awareness Campaigns

Public awareness campaigns focused on financial education issues offer a wide range of benefits for consumers. National efforts, including the distribution of public service announcements, can help educate Americans on the resources available for those in financial distress, the power and cost of money (impact of compounding from both debt and savings perspectives), and key financial concepts such as interest rates, compounding and the timetable for paying off revolving debt. In addition to a factual approach, some participants stated it may be necessary to use "shock value" to illustrate the negative outcomes such as bankruptcy and diminished quality of life.

Financial Literacy and Education Commission

Government Sector Public Meeting

Location:
Federal Deposit
Insurance Corporation (FDIC) 550 17th Street, N.W.,
Washington, D.C.,

Date:
March 4, 2005

Discussion Moderators

The discussion was moderated by Lee Bowman, FDIC, and Dan Iannicola, Treasury Department.

Discussion Participants

DAN IANNICOLA, Treasury Department
LEE BOWMAN, FDIC
RALPH AVERY, Administrative Office of the U.S. Courts
REBECCA FANNING, Administrative Office of the U.S. Courts
HILLARY HUNT, Commonwealth of Pennsylvania
DARRELL LLOYD, Internal Revenue Service
DAVID MANCL, Wisconsin Jump$tart, Coalition of Personal Finance for Youth
JERRY MUNK, National American Securities Administrator Association
ADAM RABINER, New York State Banking Department
DAPHNE SMITH, National American Securities Administrator Association
JUSTIN SOUTHERN, West Virginia State Auditor's Office
MARGARET WARREN, Internal Revenue Service
TIM MULLEN, National Association of Insurance Commissioners

Primary Focus of Meeting

Participants described several ideas for a national public awareness campaign on financial literacy. Several indicated the need for a sustained, multi-year approach, initiating a campaign that will result in lasting changes on financial behaviors. Campaign messages should be positive and empowering, particularly in the area of asset building. Messages should also be sensitive to and include different cultures, income levels, and languages. Special efforts should be made to make financial education "trendy" for both youth and adults.

Key Discussion Points

Savings and Asset Building Strategy Best Practices

Example programs cited during the meeting included Individual Development Accounts, Earned Income Tax Credit refunds, Voluntary Income Tax Assistance (VITA) sites (particularly those established as a coalition where many financial service organizations are co- located at the site), regionally focused financial institution efforts (e.g. FDIC's New Alliance Task Force in the Chicago area), and in-school bank branches.

Government's Role in Encouraging

Private Sector Involvement

While there was no consensus regarding government's role in financial education, several participants mentioned that all levels of government (Federal, state, local) should encourage various private sector professionals and organizations to volunteer time to teach financial education. Incentives such as continuing education credit or monetary incentives (seed money or tax breaks) could be provided. Workplace financial education programs, school-based branches of financial institutions, and government-sponsored events for educators would also be useful. As part of its role, government could lead the development and implementation of a centralized measurement system for determining the success of financial education initiatives.

Coordination and Management of Financial Education Programs

Participants agreed that it is paramount to better educate citizens on all financial education programs currently available in the marketplace. Keeping existing programs up to date and better promoting their available resources should be a top priority, allowing current efforts to better meet consumer needs and broaden teaching on additional financial education topics as needed.

Measuring Campaign Success

Participants identified a range of ways to measure the success of a sustained national public awareness campaign. Recommendations included monitoring the number of people who access their credit report, conducting a longitudinal study of children who had financial education and those who did not (National Bureau of Economic Research did such a study that could serve as a model), measuring the number of Individual Development Accounts and volume of matching funds and their impact, using behavioral sciences experts in the design of the metrics selected, comparing the volume of bankruptcy filings over time, conducting a before and after survey of awareness of financial scams, and considering whether there are measures within the No Child Left Behind law that might be useful in assessing levels of financial education.

Moving the Campaign Forward

First, states may consider establishing an office focused on financial literacy. This office would understand all of the organizations within the state that have a relevant piece/function related to financial education. The office would coordinate state-relevant activities and would report directly to the governor. It would be created so it does not have a general fund or taxpayer dollar implications, and could be structured on delivery systems (community-based, school-based, workplace-based, etc.) It was noted that Pennsylvania presently has such an office.

At the Federal level, the government could serve as a clearinghouse for best practices and organize and coordinate national meetings on specific topics where best practices could be shared with state and local organizations.

Financial Literacy and Education Commission Sector Meeting Summary

Education Sector Meeting

Location:
U.S. Mint,
801 9th Street, N.W., Washington, D.C.

Date:
March 7, 2005

Discussion Moderators

The discussion was moderated by Marcie Brown, Department of Education, and Dan Iannicola, Treasury Department.

Discussion Participants

DAN IANNICOLA, Treasury Department
MARCIE BROWN, Department of Education
HENRIETTA FORE, U.S. Mint
JOE BOTTA, Virginia Cooperative Extension
NORINE FULLER, Fashion Institute of Design & Merchandising
NINA TORRES, The Hispanic Association of Colleges and Universities
DEBRA MINOR DRISCOLL, Oregon State University Extension Service
ANNE FREMION, Ohio State University Extension
JOYCE LASH, Iowa State University Extension
ANGELA LYONS, University of Illinois
WAYNE MOORE, University of Missouri Extension
GAYLE ROSE MARTINEZ, University of Wisconsin
RITA STRAUB, University of Wisconsin Extension

Primary Focus of Meeting

Participants discussed various ways in which financial education resources can be disseminated to all communities throughout the country. In viewing ways to most effectively disseminate financial education, individual examples of students who lacked basic financial literacy skills were analyzed. Participants recommended the Federal government take the lead in forming partnerships that would allow financial literacy tools to reach the individuals and communities that need it most. Partnerships at all government levels, including non-government entities such as the academic community, non-profit institutions and the lending community were referenced as an extremely effective way to improve financial education.

Key Discussion Points

Government's Role in Enhancing Financial Education

Government's role in financial education should be to encourage traditional and non-traditional partnerships ranging from a broad spectrum of entities. The Federal government should bring stakeholders, especially from private and non-profit institutions, together to determine the most effective way to reach all populations and demographics. Also, several participants suggested the Department of Education partner with other Federal agencies, such as the Treasury Department, to become more involved in financial education by hosting meetings and conducting additional substantive research. Several participants also mentioned that government incentives to teach and deliver financial education tools would be greatly effective.

Measurements of Success

Measuring success was an instrument that the participants felt we needed to take time to review and suggested that the Federal government may consider that it takes time to expect results (strong results cannot happen in a short time period). The percentage of individuals filing for bankruptcy, testing after teaching financial education lessons to children, and studying the increase or decrease in retirement plan participants were all mentioned as possible indicators that the Financial Literacy and Education Commission should utilize for measuring overall effectiveness of collective efforts. In addition, it was mentioned that financial education stakeholders should look at private institutions that offer retirement planning education as part of employee orientation, versus private institutions that do not offer retirement planning education during orientation and compare the percentage of employees that choose to enroll into retirement plans. The group recognized the need for creative ways to get employee participation up in employer sponsored retirement plans.

Multimedia Public Service Campaign

Participants agreed that launching a multimedia public service campaign would be extremely effective in reaching consumers. Tailoring a message that targets specific populations and communities was emphasized. For example, when targeting young people, the campaign should focus around an area that is popular to young people, and utilize this area to focus key financial education issues. The issues of savings, individual choices and the importance of avoiding excessive debt were the key overall messages that were discussed. Portraying the beneficial effects of compound interest and offering a way to help consumers already in debt were also mentioned as essential components to developing a strong awareness campaign. Some participants suggested that educating consumers to better understand their credit scores, and to make consumers aware of the effects of a bad credit score, were key elements to empowering consumers to make better financial decisions.

Financial Education at Post-Secondary Institutions

The need to enhance financial education at colleges and universities was emphasized and several examples about students who struggled with credit card debt were given. Several of the participants pointed out that the number one reason for dropping out of school was for financial reasons, not academics. Another participant said that she personally knew two college seniors who had job offers revoked because their hiring employers did a credit check and discovered that the students had poor credit scores. Other participants mentioned that students are more likely to pay their credit card loans over their student loans.

Partnerships with schools and local banks, financial education seminars on campuses and payment courses on loans were all mentioned as possible plans that could help students make strong financial choices. Having workshops on college campuses was a suggestion that many participants supported.

Financial Literacy and Education Commission Sector Meeting Summary

Non-Profit Organization Meeting

Location:
Office of Personnel Management (OPM)
1900 E Street, NW,
Washington, D.C.

Date:
March 11, 2005

Discussion Moderators

The discussion was moderated by Marcus Beauregard, Department of Defense; Dan Iannicola, Treasury Department; and Ray Kirk, U.S. Office of Personnel Management.

Discussion Participants

DAN IANNICOLA, Treasury Department
RAY KIRK, Office of Personnel Management
MARCUS BEAUREGARD, Department of Defense
JORDANA BEEBE, Privacy Rights Clearinghouse
DON BLANDIN, Investor Protection Trust
EDWIN BODENSIEK, Junior Achievement Worldwide
DAVID CASSERLY, Jump$tart Coalition for Personal Financial Literacy
THEODORE DANIELS, Society for Financial Education
VIRGINIA DAVIS, Native Financial Education Coalition
AL DUARTE, InCharge Education Foundation Education Foundation
BOB DUVALL, National Council on Economic Education
HECTOR GAMBOA, Spanish Coalition for Housing
DAVID GODSTED, Networks Financial Institute
TRACEY GORDY, Corporation for Enterprise Development
KAREN GROSS, Coalition for Consumer Bankruptcy
JOHNETTE HARTNETT, NCB Development Corporation
SUSIE IRVINE, American Financial Services Association Education Foundation
VARINY PALADINO, American Savings Education Council
CHERYL REYNOLDS, American Institute of Certified Public Accountants
JENA ROSCOE, Operation Hope, Inc.

JAY SEATON, Consumer Credit & Counseling Service Midwest
LINDA SHERRY, Consumer Action
MAX SIMMONS, Take Charge America

Primary Focus of Meeting

Non-profit organizations recognize the need to act both nationally and locally to improve financial literacy across all audiences. Nationally, a public awareness campaign, including public service announcements, can guide discussion and generate excitement and interest among consumers. At the local level, the public, private and non-profit sectors can work together to disseminate existing resources and successfully implement best practices tailored to local community needs.

Key Discussion Points

Financial Education in the Public Schools

Participants recognized that public schools play an important role in improving financial education efforts. Participants stated that local schools can advance financial education by partnering with non-profits and government entities. Public awareness and education efforts should work in concert with each other, focusing on best practices and practical instruction. Special emphasis should be paid to providing classroom educators the professional development and support needed to integrate financial literacy into existing curricula.

Utilizing Existing Financial Education Resources

Participants stated that there are a number of specific efforts that can be undertaken to leverage existing financial education resources and coordinate outreach efforts to avoid overlap or duplication. State governments can establish offices to help shepherd the process and coordinate state-based financial education efforts. The Federal government can help bring together private, public, and non-profit organizations to encourage financial literacy activities, and the U.S. Department of Education in particular can work to facilitate the task of boosting financial skills among consumers for state and local officials. Sectors can also work together to establish a listserv to share information on best practices and to use social science mapping techniques to improve understanding on specific financial education programs.

Public Awareness Campaign

Participants agreed that a national public awareness campaign on financial literacy education is needed and would be welcomed in communities throughout the nation. Any new public engagement efforts should coordinate with existing efforts and should be carefully developed to ensure they are culturally appropriate and diverse. Public service announcements could be used to provide consumers with direct information on money management and wealth building, for instance, and identifying a popular national spokesperson was viewed as a potentially valuable component.

Measuring Success

Participants recommended that the success of financial education efforts can be measured in a number of ways, including monitoring changes in savings, investment and finance management behaviors and conducting regular town hall meetings to gather public responses. Participants recognized that success takes time, first through public awareness, then an increased level of knowledge, and finally behavior change. The first year of any education effort should focus on general awareness.

Financial Literacy and Education Commission Sector Meeting Summary

Lenders Meeting

Location:
Room H-C-8,
U.S. Capitol,
Washington, DC

Date:
March 14, 2005

Discussion Moderators

The discussion was moderated by Dan Iannicola, Treasury Department, and Barry Wides, Office of the Comptroller of the Currency.

Discussion Participants

DAN IANNICOLA, Treasury Department
BARRY WIDES, Office of the Comptroller of the Currency
THE HONORABLE DANIEL AKAKA, U.S. Senate
THE HONORABLE JUDY BIGGERT, U.S. House of Representatives
THE HONORABLE DAVID DREIER, U.S. House of Representatives
RHONDA BENTZ, Visa
KIM BOHANNON, North Carolina Credit Union League
CHRISTY MINTON, (by teleconference), Bancorp South
JODI MITCHELL, Mountain America Credit Union
CYNDY SCOTT, Tower Federal Credit Union
SHERYL NEAS, National Community Capital Association

Primary Focus of Meeting

Participants discussed the need for all sectors to work together to provide financial literacy information to consumers. As the Federal government, educators, employers, and community organizations work together to develop curricula and identify and model best practices, public service announcements and other public education efforts can be valuable in boosting consumer understanding of financial issues.

Key Discussion Points

Role of the Federal Government

Participants noted that the Federal government should engage in a range of activities to bring financial literacy to the public forefront and make it a part of the national consciousness. The Federal government can do this by providing guidance in terms of standards and best practices, encouraging and fostering partnerships across sectors, and working with state and local government to integrate financial literacy in the public schools. Most importantly, the Federal government can lend a sense of urgency to the issue of financial education that participants felt is currently absent.

Measuring Success

Participants recommended that the success of financial education efforts can be measured in many ways, including how many 401(k) plans and IRAs are used now versus 10 years from now; quantifying savings rates; decline in bankruptcies; and declines in unsecured debt; pre- and post-tests to measure effects of financial literacy curricula in public schools; increases in credit scores; and decreases in predatory lending.

Selection and Use of Programs

The Federal government can play an important role in the selection of programs by working with trusted organizations to identify current financial literacy efforts and best practices, particularly in specific states and localities. Organizations such as community colleges, credit union leagues, and the USDA Cooperative Extension Service could also play a role in evaluating current programs, and all results could be placed on a Federal Web site. Effective programs should be factual (not seen as a sales tool), and should be presented in the appropriate language and format.

Proper distribution of financial literacy education is key to its effective use.

Distribution can be accomplished through partnerships, public education, and professional development for educators. Specific efforts should also focus on providing employers with the incentives to incorporate financial education in the workplace. Employers can bring in experts to explain benefits and planning. Pastors, churches, and faith-based organizations can also play a role in the promotion of financial education.

Public Service Announcements and Public Awareness Campaigns

All public education efforts should answer the question, "What's in it for me?" Public service announcements are seen as a valuable tool in establishing a specific call to action for targeted groups (high school students, 30-year-olds, English as a Second Language individuals, etc.) To reach these audiences successfully, PSAs and other outreach efforts must be tailored; a one-size-fits-all approach will not be effective.

All public awareness products should be written at a seventh-grade reading level, with checklists and similar basic materials effectively communicating the content. Content should be simple and streamlined, as participants believe that additional background information risks getting in the way of the message.

Financial Literacy and Education Commission Sector Meeting Summary

Individual Respondents' Session

Location:

Department of Health and Human Services, Administration for Children and Families, Washington, DC

Date:

March 17, 2005

Discussion Moderators

The discussion was moderated by Dan Iannicola, Treasury Department; Luke Bernstein, Treasury Department; and Jim Gatz, Department of Health and Human Services.

Discussion Participants

DAN IANNICOLA, Treasury Department
LUKE BERNSTEIN, Treasury Department
JAMES GATZ, Health and Human Services
JIM BILELLO
KELVIN BOSTON
CATHY BOWEN
RUTH FREEMAN
KAREN HARRIS
JULIE JUDY
CHERYL MOORE
SHANNON MOYER J
ANE SCHUCHARDT
MICHAEL SCHUTT
ROBERT WEAGLEY
JUDY WEISS
ANNE YOEMAN

Primary Focus of Meeting

Raising financial literacy is a long-term process that requires multiple strategies and approaches. Successful efforts need to be developed carefully and should include specific engagement strategies and assessment mechanisms. Participants believe there are specific roles for public- and private-sector interests at the Federal, state, and local levels, and that those involved in financial literacy should understand and successfully execute their roles and capitalize on the education successes of other sectors.

Key Discussion Points

Current State and Consequences of Financial Literacy

According to participants, there is a dearth of financial skills among the population at large and among specific population subsets. More work still needs to be done to help financial institutions understand the benefits, both individually and nationally, to improving financial literacy among consumers, particularly with immigrants, families of all income brackets, small businesses, and high school and post-secondary students. The impact of such education could result in a stronger national economy, greater family self- sufficiency, and a reduction in predatory lending and reliance on the cash economy.

Existing financial literacy efforts need to focus more on measuring programmatic effectiveness. Currently, there is little knowledge on the impact of financial education on individual or institutional behavior. Participants believe the Federal government could lead an effort to identify and promote best practices in financial education initiatives, developing guidelines to evaluate the short- and long-term effects of such efforts on families and communities.

Role of the Federal Government

Participants stated that the Federal government's primary role is to identify effective financial literacy practices and promote those best practices through recognized information channels (such as MyMoney.gov). Consumers should be provided credible and useful information that specifically addresses their needs and personal situations. In addition to distributing information, the Federal government should collect, analyze and disseminate data on effective practice and design to support those implementing financial education programs at state and local levels. Targeted education efforts might focus on, for example, consumers, employers, and financial institutions, among others. The Federal government could provide incentives among Federal programs and private institutions to reward success in financial education.

Role of State and Local Institutions

Educational institutions, financial institutions, and private faith-based and community-based organizations also play an important role in increasing financial skills. Participants said state and local institutions could replicate or adapt to state and local conditions the best practices identified by the Federal government. Specific emphasis could be placed on providing financial education through the local public school system (local schools might consider instituting specific financial literacy requirements for graduation). State and local networks also could tap Cooperative Extension, colleges and universities and private financial institutions to plan, implement, and evaluate education efforts. Financial institutions could work with employers to develop local or corporate-based incentives — such as loan forgiveness, qualification for home mortgage, or lower interest rates — for achieving financial benchmarks.

Measuring Success

Participants recommended that the success of financial education efforts can be measured in a number of ways, including changes in the level of 401(k) opportunities, increased personal savings, credit repair, and the number of first-time account holders. There was strong agreement that measures of effectiveness should be realistic with respect to time and behaviors.

APPENDIX B.

52538 Federal Register / Vol. 69, No. 165 / Thursday, August 26, 2004 / Notices

The purpose of the trackage rights is to allow KO to continue to provide rail service over the subject line.

As a condition to this exemption, any employees affected by the trackage rights will be protected by the conditions imposed in *Norfolk and Western Ry. Co.—Trackage Rights—BN*, 354 I.C.C. 605 (1978), as modified in *Mendocino Coast Ry., Inc.—Lease and Operate*, 360 I.C.C. 653 (1980).

This notice is filed under 49 CFR 1180.2(d)(7). If the notice contains false or misleading information, the exemption is void *ab initio*. Petitions to revoke the exemption under 49 U.S.C. 10502(d) may be filed at any time. The filing of a petition to revoke will not automatically stay the transaction.

An original and 10 copies of all pleadings, referring to STB Finance Docket No. 34535, must be filed with the Surface Transportation Board, 1925 K Street, NW., Washington, DC 20423-0001. In addition, a copy of each pleading must be served on Craig Richey, 315 W. 3rd Street, Pittsburg, KS 66762.

Board decisions and notices are available on our Web site at *http://www.stb.dot.gov*.

Decided: August 20, 2004.

By the Board, David M. Konschnik, Director, Office of Proceedings.

Vernon A. Williams,

Secretary.

[FR Doc. 04–19529 Filed 8–25–04; 8:45 am]

BILLING CODE 4915–01–P

DEPARTMENT OF THE TREASURY

Comment Request for Financial Literacy and Education Commission National Strategy

AGENCY: Departmental Offices, Treasury.

ACTION: Request for comments.

SUMMARY: The Financial Literacy and Education Improvement Act established the Financial Literacy and Education Commission. On behalf of the Commission, the Department of the Treasury invites the public to comment on the development of a national strategy to promote the basic financial literacy and financial education of everyone in the United States.

DATES: Comments should be received on or before October 31, 2004 to be assured of consideration.

ADDRESSES: Written comments should be sent to Department of the Treasury, Financial Literacy and Education Commission, Room 5001B, 1500 Pennsylvania Avenue NW., Washington, DC 20220, or via e-mail to *flecstrategy@do.treas.gov*.

FOR FURTHER INFORMATION CONTACT: Requests for additional information should be directed to Michael Schutt at (202) 622–5770 (not a toll-free call), or by e-mail to the above address.

Additional information regarding the Commission and the Department of the Treasury's Office of Financial Education may be obtained through the Office of Financial Education's Web site at: *http://www.treas.gov/financialeducation*.

SUPPLEMENTARY INFORMATION: The Financial Literacy and Education Improvement Act, which is Title V of the Fair and Accurate Credit Transactions Act of 2003 (the "FACT Act") (Pub. L. 108–159), established the Financial Literacy and Education Commission to improve financial literacy and financial education of persons in the United States.

Request for Comments: Comments are specifically requested concerning: (1) What are the three most important issues that the national strategy should address, and why? (2) What existing resources may be used to address those issues, and how could they be employed? (3) What are the best ways to improve financial literacy and financial education in the United States? Commenters are urged to keep comments succinct and responsive to these questions.

The Commission: The Commission is chaired by the Secretary of the Treasury and is composed of the heads of the Office of the Comptroller of the Currency; the Office of Thrift Supervision; the Board of Governors of the Federal Reserve System; the Federal Deposit Insurance Corporation; the National Credit Union Administration; the Securities and Exchange Commission; the Departments of Education, Agriculture, Defense, Health and Human Services, Housing and Urban Development, Labor, and Veterans Affairs; the Federal Trade Commission; the General Services Administration; the Small Business Administration; the Social Security Administration; the Commodity Futures Trading Commission; and the Office of Personnel Management. The Commission is required, not later than 18 months after the date of enactment of the FACT Act, to develop a national strategy to promote basic financial literacy and education among all American consumers. The FACT Act was enacted on December 4, 2003.

Dated: August 20, 2004.

Dan Iannicola, Jr.,

Deputy Assistant Secretary of the Treasury.

[FR Doc. 04–19527 Filed 8–25–04; 8:45 am]

BILLING CODE 4810–25–P

DEPARTMENT OF VETERANS AFFAIRS

Disciplinary Appeals Board Panel

AGENCY: Department of Veterans Affairs.

ACTION: Notice with request for comments.

SUMMARY: Section 203 of the Department of Veterans Affairs Health Care Personnel Act of 1991 (Pub. L. 102–40), dated May 7, 1991, revised the disciplinary grievance and appeal procedures for employees appointed under 38 U.S.C. 7401(1). It also required the periodic designation of employees of the Department who are qualified to serve on Disciplinary Appeals Boards. These employees constitute the Disciplinary Appeals Board panel from which Board members in a case are appointed. This notice announces that the roster of employees on the panel is available for review and comment. Employees, employee organizations, and other interested parties shall be provided, without charge, a list of the names of employees on the panel upon request and may submit comments concerning the suitability for service on the panel of any employee whose name is on the list.

DATES: Names that appear on the panel may be selected to serve on a Board or as a grievance examiner after September 27, 2004.

ADDRESSES: Requests for the list of names of employees on the panel and written comments may be directed to: Secretary of Veterans Affairs (051E), Department of Veterans Affairs, 810 Vermont Avenue, NW., Washington, DC 20420. Requests and comments may also be faxed to (202) 273–9776.

FOR FURTHER INFORMATION CONTACT: Catherine Baranek, Employee Relations Specialist (051), Office of Human Resources Management and Labor Relations, Department of Veterans Affairs, 810 Vermont Avenue, NW., Washington, DC 20420. Ms. Baranek may be reached at (336) 631–5019.

SUPPLEMENTARY INFORMATION: Pub. L. 102–40 requires that the availability of the roster be posted in the **Federal Register** periodically, and not less than annually.

Dated: August 19, 2004.

Anthony J. Principi,

Secretary of Veterans Affairs.

[FR Doc. 04–19495 Filed 8–25–04; 8:45 am]

BILLING CODE 8320–01–M

Public Awareness Campaigns

Participants agreed that all engagement and education strategies need to be carefully tailored to consumers at large and key population subsets. Communications efforts should be positive and clear, and provide audiences with the tools and resources they need to improve financial behaviors. Any public awareness campaign should be integrated so that messages layer and reinforce each other, regardless of source and intended audience.

Efforts should be carefully planned, executed, and measured, and adjustments should be made based on campaign success. Multiple media, physical locations, and modes of access should be used to reach effectively different population subsets, including students, immigrants, older workers, rural versus urban dwellers and persons at different stages of their financial lives.

Endnotes

[1] U.S. Department of Commerce. (n.d.) *National Income and Product Accounts Table.* Retrieved July 26, 2005, from www.bea.doc.gov/bea/dn/nipaweb/TableView.asp#Mid

[2] Ibid.

[3] Greenspan, A. (2004, August 27). Remarks at the 2004 Symposium of the Federal Reserve Bank of Kansas City.

[4] National Association of Insurance Commissioners. *2003 Survey.* Retrieved from www.naic.org/ consumer_ home.htm

[5] A high deductible health plan (HDHP) is a health insurance plan with a minimum deductible of $1,000 (self-only coverage) or $2,000 (family coverage) in 2005. Annual out-of-pocket expenses (including deductibles and co-pays) cannot exceed $5,100 (self-only coverage) or $10,200 (family coverage) in 2005. HDHPs may have first dollar coverage for preventive care.

[6] U.S. Department of Agriculture. (n.d.). Cooperative State Research, Education, and Extension Service. Retrieved July 26, 2005, from http://www.csrees.usda.gov/index.html

[7] Ibid.

[8] Ibid.

[9] Bush, George W. (2001). Radio address by the President to the nation. Retrieved June 24, 2005, from http://www.whitehouse.gov/news/releases/2001/06/20010608-7.html

[10] Dietz, R.D., & Haurin, D.R. (2003). The social and private consequences of homeownership. *The Journal of Urban Economics, 54*, 401-450.

[11] The Federal Reserve Board. (2001). Survey of Consumer Finances. Retrieved from http://www. Federalreserve.gov/pubs/oss/oss2/2001/scf2001home.html.

[12] Ibid.

[13] Ibid.

[14] On April 11, 2005, Neighborhood Reinvestment Corporation began doing business as *NeighborWorks America®*. Refer to www.nw.org/network/aboutUs/history/default.asp for additional information.

[15] Neighborhood Reinvestment Corporation. (2004). Creating educated homebuyers: A Comprehensive Approach, Written Testimony before the House Committee on Financial Services, Subcommittee on Housing and Community Opportunity, Washington, DC

[16] Centers for Disease Control & Prevention. (2004, November 10). *National vital statistics reports.*

[17] Retrieved July 5, 2005, from http://www.cdc.gov/nchs/data/dvs/nvsr53_06t12.pdf

[18] Employee Benefit Research Institute. (2004). *Saving and retiring in America* (2004 RCI fact sheet). Washington, DC.

[19] U.S. Social Security Administration. (2002). *Income of the aged chartbook: 2002* (Publication 13-11727). Washington, DC.

[20] U.S. Social Security Administration. (2005). Annual report of the Board of Trustees of the Federal Old-Age and Survivors Insurance and Disability Insurance Trust Funds (p. 81). Washington, DC.

[21] Bush, George W. (2005). *The State of the Union Address.*

[22] Beller, D. *Coverage status of workers under employer provided health and pension plans.* Unpublished tabulations. Washington, DC: Employee Benefits Security Administration, Office of Policy and Research.

[23] Ibid.

[24] Purcell, P.J. (2005, September). *Pension sponsorship and participation: Summary of recent trends* (CRS Report to Congress RL30122). Washington DC: U.S. Library of Congress, Congressional Research Service.

[25] Bureau of Labor Statistics. (2005, January). *National compensation survey: Employee benefits in private industry in the United States, 2002-2003* (Bulletin 2573). Washington, DC

[26] Ibid.

[27] Hewitt Associates. *Hewitt study reveals biggest barrier to retirement saving may be lack of motivation,*" [press release]. Retrieved February 22, 2005, from http://was4.hewitt.com/hewitt/resource/newsroom/ pressrel/2005/02-22-05.htm.

[28] Sailer, P.J., & Nutter, S.E. (2000). *Accumulation and distribution of individual retirement arrangements, 2003*. Retrieved July 5, 2005, from http://irs.gov/pub/irs-soi/00retire.pdf
[29] Employee Benefit Research Institute, & Mathew Greenwald & Associates, Inc. (2005). *2005 retirement confidence survey*. Washington, DC.
[30] Ibid.
[31] Government Accountability Office, Social Security Statements. (2005, April). *Social Security Administration should better evaluate whether workers understand their statements* (GAO-05-192). Retrieved July 5, 2005, from http://www.gao.gov/highlights/d05192high.pdf.
[32] U.S. Department of Labor, Employee Benefits Security Administration. (2001). *Advisory opinion (2001-09A)*. Retrieved May 26, 2005, from http://www.dol.gov/ebsa/regs/AOs/ao2001-09a.html.
[33] Madrian, B., & Shea, D.F. (2001, November). The power of suggestion: Inertia in 401(k) participation rates and savings behavior. *Quarterly Journal of Economics. 116(4)*. Cambridge, MA. MIT Press.
[34] Vitt, L.A., et al. (2000). *Personal finance and the rush to competence: Financial literacy education in the U.S.* (A national field study commissioned and supported by the Fannie Mae Foundation). Middleburg, VA: Institute for Socio-Financial Studies.
[35] Ibid.
[36] Madrian, B. & Shea, D.F.
[37] Bernheim, B.D. (1996). *Financial literacy, education, and retirement savings*. University of Pennsylvania: Pension Research Council.
[38] Employee Benefit Research Institute, & Mathew Greenwald & Associates, Inc. (2003). *2003 Small Employer Retirement Survey*. Washington, DC: Employee Benefit Research Institute.
[39] Ibid.
[40] Ibid.
[41] U.S. Department of Labor, Employee Benefit Security Administration. Retrieved from www.dol.gov/ebsa/pdf/simplenet.pdf & www.dol.gov/ebsa/pdf/simpleIRA.pdf.
[42] Employee Benefit Research Institute, & Mathew Greenwald & Associates, Inc.
[43] Federal Reserve (n.d.). *G19 Consumer Credit*. Retrieved August 2, 2005, from www.Federalreserve.gov/releases/g19/hist/cc_hist_sa.html.
[44] American Bankruptcy Institute (n.d.). *Annual U.S. non-business bankruptcy filings by chapter 2000-2004*. Retrieved August 2, 2005, from www.abiworld.org/Template.cfm?Section=Press_Releases2&CONTENTID=12267&TEMPLATE=/ContentManagement/ContentDisplay.cf.
[45] Elliehausen, G.E., Lundquist, C., & Staten, M.E. (2003, January). *The impact of credit counseling on subsequent borrower credit usage and payment behavior*. Washington, DC: Credit Research Center, Georgetown University.
[46] Ibid.
[47] Ibid.
[48] The Government Accountability Office. (2005, March). *Credit reporting literacy: Consumers understood the basics but could benefit from targeted educational efforts* (Report GAO-05-223). Washington, DC
[49] Ibid.
[50] Many private companies and lending institutions develop scoring software systems to compute credit scores. Credit reporting agencies do not generate credit scores, but rather are repositories of consumer credit histories.
[51] The Government Accountability Office. (2005, March). *Credit reporting literacy: Consumers understood the basics but could benefit from targeted educational efforts* (Report GAO-05-223). Washington, DC: Author.
[52] Free reports are now available in all states, U.S. territories and possessions, and the District of Columbia.
[53] A credit counseling agency with 501(c)(3) status under the Internal Revenue Code is required to be organized to provide educational or charitable services, *i.e.*, it is an agency's 501(c)(3) status that requires it to provide educational services.
[54] Federal Trade Commission. (2005, March). *Facts for consumers: For people on debt management plans: A must do list*. Retrieved July 26, 2005, from www.ftc.gov/credit/.
[55] Federal Trade Commission. (2003, November). *Fiscal fitness: Choosing a credit counselor, and Knee deep in debt*. Retrieved July 26, 2005, from www.ftc.gov/credit.
[56] The "Dirty Dozen" report, published by the IRS, is an annual listing of notorious tax scams. The report also reminds taxpayers to be wary of schemes that promise to eliminate taxes or otherwise sound too good to be true. See www.irs.gov for more information.
[57] See also *Jean Chatzky (2005, August). How to find a credit counselor that you can trust*. Retrieved August 22, 2005 from www.msnbc.msn.com/id/9034211l.
[58] Federal Trade Commission. (2005, March). *Facts for consumers: Credit and your consumer rights, Federal Trade Commission*, and *Choosing a credit counselor*. Retrieved May 26, 2005, from www.ftc.gov/credit.
[59] Ibid.
[60] Federal Trade Commission (August 2004) *Consumer fraud in the United States: An FTC survey*. [Federal Trade Commission Staff Report]. Retrieved from www.ftc.gov/reports/consumerfraud/ 040805confraudrpt.pdf.
[61] Federal Bureau of Investigation (n.d.). Retrieved from: www.fbi.gov/majcases/fraud/seniorsfam. htm.

[62] Ibid.
[63] Ibid.
[64] Internal Revenue Service. (2005, March). *Internal Revenue Service Data Book 2004* (Publication 55B). Retrieved July 27, 2005, from www.irs.gov/taxstats.
[65] National Organization on Disability & Louis Harris and Associates, Inc. (2004). *N. O.D./Harris Survey of Americans with disabilities*. Washington, DC.
[66] The Florida Prosperity Plan. (n.d.). *Florida Communities Help Families Climb Out Of Poverty*. Retrieved August 2, 2005, from www.prosperitycampaign.com/floridapc.html.
[67] City of Miami. (n.d.). *City of Miami's tax preparation campaign most successful ever*. Retrieved August 2, 2005, from http://www.ci.miami.fl.us/comm/pages/Press_Release/2005_taxpreparation.asp.
[68] National Organization on Disability – Louis Harris and Associates, Inc. (2000). *N. O.D./Harris Survey of Americans with disabilities*. Washington, DC.
[67] Small Business Tax Credit: IRS Code Section 44, Disabled Access Credit.
[70] Architectural/Transportation Tax Deduction: IRS Code Section 190, Barrier Removal.
[71] Refers to an individual who has a disability that results in a substantial handicap to employment and who has been referred from a vocational rehabilitation facility.
[72] Opportunity Tax Credit: IRS Code Section 51, Work Opportunity Tax Credit (WOTC)
[73] Securities Industry Association. (November 2004). *Annual SIA investor survey*. New York, NY: Securities Industry Association Publications.
[74] Federal Trade Commission. (August 2004). *Consumer fraud in the United States: An FTC survey*. Washington, DC: Bureaus of Economics and Consumer Protection Federal Trade Commission.
[75] Braunstein, S. & Welch, C. (2002, November). *Financial literacy: An overview of practice, research, and policy* (Federal Reserve Bulletin). Washington, DC: Federal Reserve Board.
[76] Ibid.
[77] Transaction accounts form a comprehensive category comprising checking, saving and money market deposit accounts, as well as money market mutual funds and call accounts at brokerage firms. Instead of using the term "unbanked," some financial institutions may refer to these individuals as consumers in the sub-prime market or as the "underserved." For more information, see Samuels, G. (2003, Fall). *Banking unbanked immigrants through remittances*. Boston, MA: Federal Reserve Bank of Boston.
[78] Consumer Bankers Association. (2003, April). *CBA 2003 survey of bank-sponsored financial literacy programs*. Retrieved April 2003 from www.cbanet.org.
[79] Terry, D.F. (in press). Remittances as a development tool. In D.F. Terry & S.R. Wilson (Eds.), *Beyond small change: Making migrant remittances count*. Washington, D.C: Inter-American Development Bank.
[80] Frumkin, S. (2005, September). *Remittances: A gateway to banking for unbanked immigrants*. Office of the Comptroller of the Currency, Community Developments Insights. Retrieved May 26, 2005, from www.occ.treas.gov/cdd/Remittances1.pdf.
[81] Federal Deposit Insurance Corporation (FDIC). (2005, January). *FDIC and IRS partner in promoting access and financial education to workers eligible for earned income tax credits*. (Press Release). Retrieved July 27, 2005, from www.fdic.gov/consumers/consumer/moneysmart/press/2005/mspr105.html.
[82] Federal Deposit Insurance Corporation (FDIC). (2002, April). *FDIC and Neighborhood Reinvestment Corporation announce program to promote financial education and homeownership* (Press Release) Retrieved from www.fdic.gov/news/news/press/2002/pr4202.html.
[83] Riddle, Julie. (personal communications) (n.d.). Retrieved July 27, 2005, from www. thefamilyconservancy.org/life/fab.htm Connell, Kelly Moema. (personal communications) (n.d.). Retrieved July 27, 2005, from www.elcentroinc.com/english/special_initiatives/programs_soon. html.
[84] For more information on IDAs, see Office of the Comptroller of the Currency, Community Developments Insights. (2005, February). *Individual Development Accounts: An Asset Building Product for Lower-Income Consumers*. Howard, S. and Frumkin, S. Retrieved from: www.occ.treas.gov/ftp/ release/2005-25a.pdf or www.acf.hhs.gov/assetbuilding/about.html.
[85] Selig Center for Economic Growth, University of Georgia. (2004, Third Quarter). The multicultural economy 2004: America's minority buying power. (*Georgia Business and Economic Conditions, 63)*(3). Retrieved July 27, 2005, from www.selig.uga.edu/forecast/GBEC/GBEC043Q.pdf
[86] Ibid.
[87] Berry, Michael B. (Ed.). (2004, October). Financial access for immigrant's conference: Learning from diverse perspectives (Special issue). [Electronic version]. *Profitwise News and Views*. Retrieved July 27, 2005, from www.chicagofed.org/community_development/files/10_2004_pnv_session.pdf
[88] U.S. Census Bureau, (2005, April 25). *Census Bureau Reports on Residential Vacancies and Homeownership*. Retrieved August 2, 2005, from www.census.gov/hhes/www/housing/hvs/ qtr105/q105prss.pdf
[89] U.S. Census Bureau, www.census.gov/hhes/www/housing/hvs/annual04/ann04t20.html
[90] Frias, M. (2004, Winter). Linking international remittance flows to financial services: Tapping the Latino immigrant market. *Supervisory Insights*, 22-23. Retrieved from: www.fdic.gov/regulations/ examinations/supervisory/insights/siwin04/latino_mkt.html

[91] Orozco, Manuel. (2004). *The Remittance Marketplace: Prices, Policy and Financial Institutions* (Pew Hispanic Center Report). Washington, DC: Georgetown University. Institute for the Study of Internal Migration.
[92] Frias, M. (2004,Winter).
[93] Neighborhood Reinvestment Corporation, The NeighborWorks America® Network, and the NeighborWorks America® Campaign for Homeownership 2002. (2001) *Winning Strategies: Best Practices in the Work of Homeownership Promotion*. Washington, DC: Neighborhood Reinvestment Corporation.
[94] Greenspan, Alan (2005, April 8). *The Federal Reserve System's fourth annual community affairs research conference*, Washington, DC: The Federal Reserve Board.
[95] The National Council on Economic Education. (2005, March). *The standards in economics survey: What American teens & adults know about economics*. New York, NY.
[96] Jump$tart Coalition® for Personal Financial Literacy. (2004). *2004 personal financial survey of high school seniors*. Washington, D.C.
[97] Ibid.
[98] Ibid.
[99] Ibid.
[100] Ibid.
[101] Ibid.
[102] National Center for Education Statistics. (2002, November). *Short-term enrollment in postsecondary education: Student background and institutional differences in reasons for early departure, 1996–98* (NCES 2003–153). Washington, DC: U.S. Department of Education, Office of Educational Research and Improvement. Retrieved August 4, 2005, from: nces.ed.gov/pubs2003/2003153.pdf.
[103] U.S. Department of the Treasury, Office of Financial Education. (October 2002). *Integrating financial education into school curricula: Giving America's youth the educational foundation for making effective financial decisions throughout their lives by teaching financial concepts as part of math and reading curricula in elementary, middle, and high schools* (White Paper). Washington, DC.
[104] Data from U.S. Department of Agriculture, Cooperative State Research, Education, and Extension Service.
[105] U.S. Department of Education, National Center for Education Statistics. (2001) *Beginning postsecondary students longitudinal study*. Washington, D.C.
[106] The Government Accountability Office. (2004, November). *The Federal government's role in improving financial literacy* (Report GAO-05-93-SP). Washington, DC.
[107] Vitt, L.A., et al. (2003). *Personal finance and the rush to competence: Financial literacy education in the U.S: A national field study commissioned and supported by the Fannie Mae Foundation*. Middleburg, VA: Institute for Socio-Financial Studies.
[108] Ibid.
[109] Barron, J.M., & Staten, M.E. (2004). Usage of credit cards received through college student- marketing programs. *NASFAA Journal of Student Financial Aid, 34*(3).
[110] Bernheim, B.D. (1996). *Financial literacy, education, and retirement savings*. University of Pennsylvania: Pension Research Council.
[111] Clancy, N., Grinstein-Weiss, M., & Schreiner M. (2001). *Financial education and savings outcomes in Individual Development Accounts*. Washington University in St. Louis: Center for Social Development.
[112] Hira, T.K. (2005). Understanding the impact of employer-provided financial education on workplace satisfaction. *Journal of Consumer Affairs, 39*(1).
[113] Clark, R.L., & d-Ambrosia, M.B. (2003). *Ignorance is not bliss: The importance of financial education*. North Carolina State University and TIAA-CREF Institute.
[114] Bernheim, B.D., & Garrett, D.M. (1996). *The determinants and consequences of financial education in the workplace: Evidence from a survey of households*. Cambridge, MA: National Bureau of Economic Research.
[115] Bernheim, B.D., Garrett, D.M., & Maki, D.M. (1997). *Education and savings: The long-term effects of high school financial curriculum mandates*. Cambridge, MA: National Bureau of Economic Research.
[116] *ANZ Survey of adult financial literacy* [Final report]. (2003, May) Melbourne, Victoria: Roy Morgan Research.

Chapter Sources

The following chapters have been previously published

Chapter 1. – This is an edited, reformatted and augmented version of a National Literacy and Education Commission publication dated April 2006.

Chapter 2. – This is an edited, reformatted and augmented version of a United States Government Accountability Office publication 09-638ST dated April 2009.

Chapter 3. – This is an edited, reformatted and augmented version of a National Literacy and Education Commission publication dated April 2007.

INDEX

D

E

F

G

H

I

J

K

L

M

N

O

P

Q

R

S

T

U

V

W

Y